THE PURPOSE OF MAN

A.W. TOZER

Compiled and Edited by JAMES L. SNYDER

THE

PURPOSE

OF

MAN

DESIGNED TO WORSHIP

Regal

From Gospel Light
Ventura, California, U.S.A.

Published by Regal
From Gospel Light
Ventura, California, U.S.A.
www.regalbooks.com
Printed in the U.S.A.

Library of Congress Cataloging-in-Publication Data
Tozer, A. W. (Aiden Wilson), 1897-1963.
The purpose of man : designed to worship / A.W. Tozer ;
compiled and edited by James L. Snyder.
p. cm.
ISBN 978-0-8307-4689-7 (trade paper)
1. Worship. I. Snyder, James L. II. Title.
BV10.3.T69 2009
248.3—dc22
2008032295

Rights for publishing this book outside the U.S.A. or in
non-English languages are administered by Gospel Light Worldwide,
an international not-for-profit ministry. For additional information,
please visit www.glww.org, email info@glww.org, or write to
Gospel Light Worldwide, 1957 Eastman Avenue,
Ventura, CA 93003, U.S.A.

CONTENTS

A. W. Tozer: A Heart to Worship

For more than 44 years, Aiden Wilson Tozer served as a minister in the Christian and Missionary Alliance. His most prominent ministry was 31 years at the Southside Alliance Church in Chicago, often referred to as that citadel of Fundamentalism. His ministry, however, went beyond the confines of a denomination. He served as a voice to the entire Body of Christ. His books and articles were eagerly read, and his conference ministry attended with great expectation. Rarely did he disappoint those who knew him. If you were looking for formulaic Christianity, you were disappointed with him. If you were interested in what he referred to as "feel good Christianity," you were greatly disappointed.

During his life, Tozer earned a reputation for many things: an outspoken critic of the religious scene, an outstanding preacher, editor of a leading Christian periodical and author of several devotional classics. The real focus, however, of his daily life centered on the worship of God. Nothing else so occupied his mind and life. This worship of God was not something tacked on to a busy schedule. It became the one great passion of his life. Everything revolved around his personal worship of God.

Worship as a Lifestyle

Tozer paid the price for this lifestyle of worship. Many, even of his own family, did not understand him and his insistence on being alone. Some even regarded him as a bit odd; but what others thought of him did not trouble him in the least. His primary business was the worship of God. Nothing else mattered more than that.

To appreciate the ministry of Tozer, you must comprehend his passion for worship. If not, you will likely misunderstand not only his words, but his actions as well. He was completely committed to this one solemn activity and pursued it with all the passion he had. Tozer's ideas regarding worship were hammered into conviction that governed his life and ministry. "Worship," Tozer explained, "is to feel in your heart and express in some appropriate manner a humbling but delightful sense of admiring awe and astonished wonder and overpowering love in the presence of that most ancient Mystery, that majesty which philosophers call the First Cause but which we call Our Father Which Art in Heaven."

Tozer walked to the beat of a different drummer, but it was not simply because he was a rebel. That may have been a small part of it, but the main factor was his complete sellout to Jesus Christ. Family, friends and even the ministry had to take a back seat to this yearning of his. Perhaps his essay "The Saint Must Walk Alone" explains to a certain degree his idea of true spirituality. His focus in life was on the person of Jesus Christ, and he would do everything within his power to sharpen that focus. All his spiritual energies and disciplines were directed in that singular path. Consequently, in a certain degree, he was difficult to live with, not because he was demanding or irascible, but because he was simply focused on God.

At times, he would come to the family dinner table, especially after the children had left home, and not speak a word. He wasn't mad at anyone; he was focused on God, and would not break the focus even for fellowship around the table with friends and family. Tozer did not spend too much time working on his social graces, probably one glaring weakness in his character. Yet, to do the work he believed God called him to demanded much time away from people and shut up alone with God.

Tozer daily cultivated the ability to focus on God. He would quiet his heart, and out of that quietness would come adoration and worship for the triune Godhead.

Often at conferences, Tozer seemed preoccupied. He was always musing on some aspect of God. He once claimed that he had dreams of God, so much were his thoughts directed toward the Godhead. Although quite knowledgeable on a variety of subjects, and with strong opinions on many of them, in later life, Tozer's focus on God got sharper and he disengaged from most other subjects to the exclusion of worship.

The lessons Tozer learned in worship he generously shared with all who would listen. His preaching and writing were simply the clear declarations of what he had experienced in his private sessions with God. Emerging from his prayer closet, dripping with the fragrance of the Presence, he was eager to report all he had witnessed. After such a sermon during his Chicago ministry, one in the congregation observed, "He out-Davided David."

A Message for the Generations

Few writers get to the heart of a subject as quickly as Tozer. He bypassed the trivia and concentrated on those essential ingredients important to the believer's walk with God. In this book, he bares his soul on worship—the one great obsession of his life. Though many have written about worship, I believe that Tozer surpasses them all in simple passion and supreme purpose. A reader coming away from this book will not only understand worship but will also experience it in his or her own heart.

You may not always agree with him, but you will always know what he believes and why. He says, "This will be the best teaching in my ministry, comparing myself with myself." The ensuing messages prove Tozer to be the prophet his reputation suggests. "I want to deliver my soul as a prophet of God to the people, and to explain why we were created and why we are here, not to the satisfaction of the immediate appetite only but to something bigger, grander and more eternal, that we might worship God and enjoy Him forever."

Throughout this book, Dr. Tozer systematically presents his teaching on a subject close to his heart. Nowhere will anyone find a more fully developed thesis on worship with such sanctified passion. Tozer was one of the first in evangelical circles to call attention to this neglected Bible doctrine. He issued a clarion call for Christians to return to their first love. Now that the pendulum has swung to the other extreme in the evangelical church, these teachings are as needed today as when Tozer first preached them.

Many people are interested in the subject of worship, and most books focus on technology and performance. Here is a book deeply rooted in Bible doctrine and historic writings that focus on the Presence of God. One of the great aspects of this book is how Tozer blends Scripture with some of the great devotional writers throughout history. Many refer to these as Mystics, and Tozer is responsible for introducing these great saints to Protestants and evangelicals. The book is well seasoned with the thoughts of these great saints of the past and their Spirit-inspired writings.

A close study of Tozer's ministry will warrant the simple conclusion that his ministry was not just cranking out sermons, articles and editorials. He always had something significant to report. His entire ministry was marked with this distinction. He firmly believed that his labor must flow from a life of worship. Any work that does not flow from worship is unacceptable to God. And, after all, it is God we are trying to please, not man.

Throughout his long ministry, Tozer never became entangled in social or political issues. Not that he did not have an opinion on these subjects, for he did. His conviction was that he was responsible to stick to the great essentials of life. That is why his writings today are just as fresh and relevant as when first published. He believed that certain things never change, whatever the generation. He kept to those fundamentals, and you either loved what Tozer said or hated it. While other ministers were becoming involved in political issues, Tozer contented himself with preaching about God.

In this book on worship, Tozer's purpose is twofold: to deliver his soul on a subject close to his heart and to inspire others to cultivate a spirit of worship in daily living. Tozer lays a solid foundation here, and once a person has read this book, he can go on to develop a lifestyle of worship that dominates his life. No one who reads this book all the way through will be the same as before, especially when it comes to his or her personal worship of God.

Often, when in a thoughtful mood, Tozer confided to a friend, "My ambition is to love God more than any one of my generation." Whatever he meant by that, it is evident that he possessed a passion for God that controlled everything in his life. Some evidence exists suggesting he achieved his goal more than he imagined.

The first book he wrote that brought him to the attention of the Christian public was *The Pursuit of God*. The last book was *The Knowledge of the Holy*. Tozer lived between these two books. Tozer *lived* a lifestyle of worship, and nothing else truly mattered to him. He sacrificed family, friends and reputation in his pursuit of God.

Tozer's criticism of entertainment within the church made him quite infamous during his lifetime. At times, his high view of worship caused him to lash out mercilessly. Worship was to be pure and untainted by worldly things. In his mind, the two were opposed to each other. When someone suggested that singing a hymn was a form of entertainment, it riled Tozer's fury. Some of his most eloquent denunciations were in this direction. He was justly concerned about the inroads worldliness was making in the Church, and its effect on Christians. Especially was he adamant about contemporary evangelism methods that many were advocating. He felt it lowered the standards of the Church, and he was dead set against it.

His comments at times are sharp because of his deep love for the Church and the fellowship of God's people. He did not relish the idea of any compromise with the message or the spirit of New Testament Christianity. He truly believed that the Church of Jesus Christ had a viable message for the world and he was anxious that the message not be mixed or diluted. Desperate times require strong medicine, and Tozer felt that the Church was backing away from her strong medicine and becoming adjusted to the world around.

He aptly described his philosophy when he said, "I believe everything is wrong until God sets it right." This is where he began; and from that position, he proclaimed freedom through the Lord Jesus Christ.

Entertainment in the Church

Tozer once wrote a booklet, "The Menace of the Religious Movie," in which he set forth in irresistible logic his conviction on the matter of entertainment in the church. The opinions are strong yet backed by biblical principles. Not only must the message please God but the methods of getting that message out must please God and be compatible with the character and nature of God. He continually ridiculed the idea that "new days demand new ways."

To appreciate fully Tozer's criticism of entertainment, his idea of worship must be examined. He firmly believed that entertainment would undermine Christian worship and put the Church in jeopardy, a thought abhorrent to Tozer. The integrity of the church, as Tozer saw it, was in danger of being compromised by the introduction of "things" into the sanctuary. His ideas of music, prayer, evangelism and missions sprang from the imperative of worship within the Christian community.

Tozer's Spiritual Legacy

The legacy of Tozer is in the area of *the majesty of God*. Whatever else Tozer did, his supreme desire was to exalt the Lord Jesus Christ as simply as possible. He tried to set before his generation the importance of certain virtues, such as simplicity and solitude, and to turn the attention of the young preachers, for he had a great influence among them, away from sham and pretense and all kinds of flesh that could creep into church politics. Getting alone with your Bible and a hymnal was highly recommended by Tozer. It was this intimacy with God that made his ministry what it became and is remembered now.

Another significant aspect of his legacy is *spiritual insight*. Tozer saw into the nature of things so deeply that it burdened him. He once made the remark that if you want to be happy, do not pray for discernment. Tozer had the gift of spiritual discernment. He could see beyond the present action to the impending result in the years to come. He could see that the way the evangelical church of his day was going, it soon would be in serious spiritual trouble. His message was always to turn back to God despite the inconvenience or cost. He urged churches to forget the Madison Avenue techniques, the strategies of the world and their programs and priorities. He advocated a life of sacrifice, self-denial and service for Christ.

During his lifetime, Tozer was widely recognized as a spokesman for God. His insight into spiritual matters was penetratingly accurate. He was widely read, but rarely followed. Those who did have the courage to follow discovered, to their delight, spiritual realities surpassing anything this world has to offer. And once experienced, it is difficult to go back to the religious boredom of the average Christian.

Tozer usually directed his ministry toward the common Christian. His message could be understood by the common person in the pew, but the average Christian, delighting in mediocrity, took no delight in his pronouncements and spiritual ardor. It was once said of St. Augustine, Bishop of Hippo, that he was a radical Christian. Such could be said of A. W. Tozer.

In his prayers, Tozer never feigned a sanctimonious posture but maintained a continuous sense of God that enveloped him in reverence and adoration. His one daily exercise was the practice of the presence of God, pursuing Him with all his time and energy. To him, Jesus Christ was a daily wonder, a recurring astonishment, a continual amazement of love and grace.

"If you major on knowing God," Tozer once wrote, "and cultivate a sense of His presence in your daily life, and do what Brother Lawrence advises, 'Practice the presence of God' daily and seek to know the Holy Spirit in the Scriptures, you will go a long way in serving your generation for God. No man has any right to die until he has served his generation."

Correct doctrine was not enough for Tozer. "You can be," Tozer delighted in saying, "straight as a gun barrel theologically and as empty as one spiritually." His emphasis was always on a personal relationship with God; a relationship so real, so personal and so overpowering as to utterly captivate a person's full attention. He longed for what he termed a God-conscious soul, a heart aflame for God.

The lack of spirituality among men and women today is embarrassingly evident. Tozer zeroed in on one of the primary causes. "I am convinced," Tozer said, "that the dearth of great saints in these times even among those who truly believe in Christ is due at least in part to our unwillingness to give sufficient time to the cultivation of the knowledge of God." He went on to develop this further. "Our religious activities should be ordered in such a way as to leave plenty of time for the cultivation of the fruits of solitude and silence."

There were times when Tozer stood alone on certain issues, which never intimidated him in the least. He never concerned himself about who stood with him on any issue. His concern was always with the truth. He was fearless in his denunciation, which made enemies rather quickly. He once criticized a popular new Bible translation. "Reading that new translation," opined Tozer, "gave me the same feeling a man might have if he tried to shave with a banana."

People waited upon Tozer's ministry with expectancy, knowing that they would hear old truths robed in fresh and sparkling, sometimes startling expressions. Tozer once said, "Years ago, I prayed that God would sharpen my mind and enable me to receive everything He wanted to say to me. I then prayed that God would anoint my head with the oil of the prophet so I could say it back to the people. That one prayer has cost me plenty since, I can tell you that."

Raymond McAfee, Tozer's assistant for more than 15 years, regularly met in Tozer's study each Tuesday, Thursday and Saturday morning for a half hour of prayer. Often when McAfee would enter, Tozer would read aloud something he recently had been reading—it might be from the Bible, a hymnal, a devotional writer or a book of poetry. Then he would kneel by his chair and begin to pray. At times, he prayed with his face lifted upward. Other times he would pray prostrate on the floor, a piece of paper under his face to keep him from breathing carpet dust.

McAfee recalls one especially memorable day. "Tozer knelt by his chair, took off his glasses and laid them on the chair. Resting on his bent ankles, he clasped his hands together, raised his face with his eyes closed and began: 'O God, we are before Thee.' With that, there came a rush of God's presence that filled the room. We both worshiped in silent ecstasy and wonder and adoration. I've never forgotten that moment, and I don't want to forget it."

In prayer, Tozer would shut out everything and everyone and focus on God. His Mystic mentors taught him that. They showed him how to practice daily the presence of God. He learned the lesson well.

The primary emphasis of Tozer's ministry in preaching and writing was in this area of worship. To him, worship is the Christian's full-time occupation. Nothing should be allowed to interfere or diminish this sacred duty of the believer. According to Tozer, whatever did not flow naturally, if not spontaneously, out of our worship was not authentic and was at best contrived. Only cunning works of silver and gold should be offered to God.

Almost as a lone voice in his generation, Tozer stressed the need for a drastic reform of worship, both personally and congregationally, and that our ideas of worship must be in complete harmony with the revealed Word of God.

During the 1950s, Tozer found a kindred spirit in a plumber from Ireland, Tom Haire, a lay preacher. Haire became the subject of seven articles Tozer wrote for *Alliance Life* entitled "The Praying Plumber from Lisburn," later reissued as a booklet. Two men could hardly have been more different, yet their love for God and their sense of His worth drew them together.

Once, while Haire was visiting Chicago, Tozer's church was engaged in a night of fasting and prayer. Haire joined them. In the middle of the night, he got thirsty and went out for a cup of tea. Some church members felt that Tom, by so doing, had "yielded to the flesh." Tozer disagreed. He saw in that act the beautiful liberty Tom enjoyed in the Lord.

Just before Haire was to return to his homeland, he stopped by Chicago to say good-bye.

"Well, Tom," Tozer remarked, "I guess you'll be going back to Ireland to preach."

"No," Tom replied in his thick Irish brogue. "I intend to cancel all appointments for the next six months and spend that time preparing for the judgment seat of Christ while I can still do something about it."

It was an attitude not uncharacteristic of Tozer himself.

If this book drives you to your knees in penitential worship before God and encourages you to withdraw from the rat race of religious life and focus on your birthright of worship, it will be well worth the pains of publication.

—James Snyder

DESIGNED TO WORSHIP

THE TRAGEDY OF HUMAN DEPRAVITY

My heart is inditing a good matter: I speak of the things which I have made touching the king: my tongue is the pen of a ready writer. Thou art fairer than the children of men: grace is poured into thy lips: therefore God hath blessed thee for ever. Gird thy sword upon thy thigh, O most mighty, with thy glory and thy majesty. And in thy majesty ride prosperously because of truth and meekness and righteousness; and thy right hand shall teach thee terrible things. Thine arrows are sharp in the heart of the king's enemies; whereby the people fall under thee.

PSALM 45:1-5

In the beginning, God created Adam and Eve, placing them in the beautiful garden east of Eden. We have only a little glimpse into the beauty of that mysterious and wondrous world. All we know is that God created it and afterwards said, "It is good," meaning that all creation was in absolute harmony with God and fulfilling its ordained purpose.

Perhaps it would be correct to suggest that many people in their frantic pursuit of life have forgotten the purpose of their creation, from God's point of view. Keep in mind that whatever

God created, He created for His purpose and pleasure (see Rev. 4:11). To entertain the idea that God would do anything capriciously or without purpose is to misunderstand completely the nature of God.

After God had created everything else, He said with a smile on His face, "I'll make me a man." Stooping down, He took up the clay from the bed of the river, shaped it and worked on it like a nanny bending over her baby. He shaped and formed man and blew into his nostrils the breath of life, and man became a living soul. God stood man upon his feet and said, "Look around, this is all yours; and look at Me, I am yours; and I'll look at you and I'll see in your face the reflection of My own glory. That is your end, that is why you were created, that you might worship Me and enjoy Me and glorify Me and have Me as yours forever."

God then put Adam into a deep sleep, and out of his ribs formed woman, whom Adam called Eve. Together they were created with one purpose.

God's purpose in creating Adam and Eve is summed up in what they could do for God that nothing else in the whole creation could do. They had an exclusive on God shared by no other of God's creation. Unlike everything else in this mystic and marvelous world of God's creation, Adam and Eve could worship God, and God anticipated that worship. In the cool of the day, God came down and walked with Adam and Eve in the Garden of Eden where they joyously offered their reverence and adoration. Nowhere do we read that God came down and hugged a tree or walked with any animal or plant He created, nor did He talk to any of the animals. Only Adam and Eve were able to provide the fellowship God desired. It was their unique purpose shared by nothing else in all of God's creation.

Thinking of those occasions of God walking with them in the cool of the day in the garden, I wonder what they talked about. The weather was ideal; Adam and Eve enjoyed perfect health; and sports had not been invented. Obviously, it was a fellowship based upon compatibility between both parties. Something in man responded to the presence of God like nothing else in all God's creation. God created man in His own image, and out of that flowed the marvelous dynamic of worship. Adam and Eve's unique purpose in the garden was to bring pleasure, joy and fellowship to God, which is the foundation of all genuine worship.

Everything in the garden was in perfect harmony and symmetry. Then God withdrew for a moment and, while gone, that old, evil one, the dragon who is called Satan, came and sowed poisonous seed in the mind of Adam and Eve. Consequently, they rebelled against God and His purpose for them. When Adam and Eve crossed the line, immediately God knew the fellowship was broken, for God knows all things.

Fig-Leaf Religion

Also, for Adam and Eve, there was a terrific sense of disorientation resulting in spiritual amnesia. They looked at themselves for the first time and saw themselves in a different light. They saw their nakedness and, in a state of spiritual disorientation, gathered fig leaves to hide their nakedness. Thus was born religion: Fig-Leaf Religion. Religion always focuses on the externals, and Adam and Eve were consumed with their outward condition. They had lost the focus of their inward beauty and purpose, and no longer satisfied the criteria of fellowship with their Creator.

When God came as usual for His fellowship, Adam and Eve were nowhere to be found; and God sought them among the trees in the garden, and called out to Adam, "Where art thou?"

God called out to the man who had fled from Him and hid out among the trees of the garden. Adam heard the voice of the Lord in the cool of the day as before, but Adam was confused. Why was God coming to Eden eastward? What was He doing there? He was coming for His customary time with Adam when Adam should worship, admire and adore the God who made him.

Adam, shamefaced, came crawling out from behind some tree. God asked, "What did you do?"

Adam regretfully replied, "We ate of the forbidden fruit." Then to justify his actions, he said, "But it was the woman you gave me."

God turned to the woman. "What did you do?" Immediately she put the blame on the serpent.

Already they had learned to blame somebody else for the condition of their soul. This blaming someone else for all our iniquities is one of the great evidences of sin and is the forerunner of religion.

Something happened, changing the whole scenario, hijacking and barring humanity from the knowledge of God. Adam and Eve, in that perfect environment and with their one supreme purpose of worshiping God, rebelled against their purpose, resulting in what theologians call the Fall of man, or Depravity.

Our world is full of tragedy because of this great, overwhelming cosmic tragedy back in the Garden. Repercussions still vibrate in contemporary society.

The burning question needing an answer is what was the tragic consequence of this Fall? Why does this matter for us today, and why should we inquire into it?

Some say the Fall is the source of all the problems plaguing humanity down through the years. Some point to the proliferation of disease as a direct outcome. Others point to all of the hatred infecting humanity throughout the centuries: nation rising against nation, kingdom against kingdom and holocausts that have happened periodically throughout history. No generation has escaped such hatred and anger. However, these are short-term effects and simply a consequence not representing the real tragedy of the Fall.

Purpose Lost

What was the real tragedy of that dreadful cosmic rupture forever affecting mankind? The real tragedy in the Garden of Eden was that Adam and Eve lost their purpose. They forgot who they were. They did not know where they were; they did not understand where they came from or what they were here for. They forgot the purpose of their existence. Trying their best to shake off this moral fog, they could not; for no matter what they did, it would not shake. Therefore, hand in hand, they made their way out into the world, not knowing where they were going. Humanity still wanders in this moral and spiritual wilderness.

They suffered from what I will refer to as spiritual amnesia. This spiritual morass is illustrated, as is often the case, in the physical world. A man wakes up in the hospital only to discover that he has been in a coma for about a week. He does not know how he got there or why he is there. He does not know where he is; in fact, he cannot even remember his name. He is told that over a week ago he encountered muggers who beat him severely, robbing him of everything, including his identity. Anything to tell who he was or why he was in the city was stripped from him. The doctors diagnosed him with amnesia. It is a real problem, because the man has no memory of what happened to him. He has lost all perspective of his life, not even knowing his own name, making him vulnerable to people he does not know.

This identity crisis is a serious condition and, thankfully, for many people it is only temporary. With the diligent work and patient help of the medical staff, memory can be restored. But until he regains his memory, he has lost all purpose in life and must rely on others to help him define his purpose.

This is the way that it is spiritually. Because the enemy of man's soul has mugged humanity, robbing them of their identity, men and women wander around in a spiritual and moral fog, not knowing who they are, what they are or where they are going.

This is exactly where humanity is today. We have a strange spiritual amnesia and cannot remember who we are or why we are here, and we look around for some explanation of our existence. Unfortunately, men and women suffering from this seek answers from anyone offering some hope. Too often, they get the wrong answers from those with less credible integrity, not to mention personal agenda.

Ask a young university graduate, "Bob, why are you here?"

"I want to get married; I'd like to make money; and I'd like to travel."

"But listen, Bob, those are shortsighted things. You will do them and then you will get old and die. What is the big overriding purpose of your life?"

Looking rather strangely, Bob might say, "I don't know whether I have any purpose in life."

This is the condition of the world today, everywhere and in every culture. From the universities to the coal mines, people do not know why they are here. People have a strange moral and spiritual amnesia and do not know their purpose in life, why they were created or what they are sent to do. Consequently, lives are filled with confusion, reaching out for any explanation; hence the proliferation of religions in our world. Religion only addresses man's external condition, not his internal confusion.

In spite of this confusion, we try to get around somehow. We travel, play golf, drive cars, eat, sleep, look at beautiful things; but they are all shortsighted aspects of our life.

The enemy of man's soul has successfully sabotaged this search for moral and spiritual identity. He does everything within his extensive power to prevent us from discovering who and what we are. Defiantly, knowing our purpose, he stands between us and dares us to cross his line. He offers everything and anything to keep us from finding the right solution. Unfortunately, he has many takers.

Where in the world can we find any answer to this dilemma? What authority in this world can bring us to an understanding of why we are here?

Fortunately for us, the Bible is such an authority and explains to us why we are here.

Purpose Regained

I desire to deliver my soul as a prophet of God and explain from the Bible why we were created and why we are here. It may not satisfy the temporary needs at the time, but it will satisfy something bigger, grander and more eternal. *That biblically defined purpose is that we might worship God and enjoy Him forever.* Apart from that, man has no other purpose; and short of that, man wanders in a spiritual disorientation taking him further from finding his created purpose.

God never does anything without a good purpose behind it. God is intelligent because intellect is an attribute of deity. This intellect is seen in every aspect of creation. Nothing in creation is without meaning, even if we do not see or understand the meaning at the time.

Deep within the heart of every person is an insatiable longing to know this purpose of life, which I contend, is indication of the residue of memory prior to the Fall in the Garden of Eden. Men and women strive to know the "why" of everything. They express a legitimate concern and pose an important question demanding a satisfactory answer. The problem is, most people get the wrong answer to their inquiry.

But there is a good and legitimate answer to this query, summed up in the following Scripture: "My heart is inditing a good matter; I speak of the things . . . touching the king. . . . So shall the king greatly desire thy beauty: for he is thy Lord; and worship thou him" (Ps. 45:1,11).

And I could go farther over into the psalms: "O come, let us worship and bow down: let us kneel before the LORD our maker" (Ps. 95:6) and Psalm 96.

Additionally, I could turn to many more passages of sacred Scripture offering to all mankind a call to worship. It is the echo of the voice of worship telling us why we were born: that we might worship God and enjoy Him forever. It is informing us that we are to glorify Him forever and, above all other creatures, know, admire, love and adore the triune God. We are to give to God that which He desires.

In our Bibles, we read of those who worship God day and night in the temple and never cease chanting, "Holy, holy, holy, is the LORD of hosts, the whole earth is full of his glory" (Isa. 6:3).

Compare this with the average run-of-the-mill church, even today's evangelical church, where there seems to be a great love of everything but this. What passes for worship in many churches today is anything and everything but what reflects the holy mind and nature of God or even pleases God. Worship in many cases is stiff and artificial, with no semblance of life in it. I am afraid that many have truly forgotten what it means to worship God in the sacred assembly. There is ritual and routine aplenty but lacking the overwhelming passion of being in the holy presence of God.

Some say the answer to all our problems in the church today is revival, as though that is a panacea for all our spiritual ills and shortcomings. Most people's idea of revival, however, runs the gamut of a week of meetings to a high-energy display of emotionalism. What is real revival? It's the kind that has changed the course of human history. Throughout church history, every revival resulted in a sudden intensification of the presence of God, resulting in the spontaneous worship of God. Anything less is superficial, artificial and even detrimental to true spiritual health.

When the Holy Ghost came on the Day of Pentecost, why did the believers break out into ecstatic language? Simply, it was because they were rightly worshiping God for the first time. Intensive worship unexpectedly leaped out of their hearts. It was nothing planned or perpetrated by some "worship leader." God was in their midst. Whenever there is a move of the Holy Spirit, it is always a call for God's people to be worshipers of the Most High God above everything else. Whatever else revival does, it must restore the purpose and meaning of being a worshiper.

In the world created by God, nothing exists without meaning and purpose. Science seeks to discover the meaning of things and their relationship to each other, their interaction and effect upon each other. That is science; I have nothing against science. However, science and scientists only deal with short-term affairs, never with the overarching purpose with man created in the image of God.

Admittedly, science has made great strides in eliminating some diseases that in a former generation took the lives of thousands. And for this, we all stand with head bowed and utter profuse thanks.

I grant you that science, especially medical science, has made great improvements in the quality of our life. But even that has limitations. Science can save a baby from diphtheria,

THE TRAGEDY OF HUMAN DEPRAVITY

save a teen from smallpox, save a person in his twenties from polio, save a man in his fifties from a heart attack and keep him right on going with good health until he is 90. But the question I pose is this: If he still does not know why he is here, what does he gain?

If he does not know why he is here and does not know his purpose, all you are doing is simply perpetuating the life without direction or purpose. If a person is living just because it is the best alternative to dying, what good is it?

Somebody observed about Christopher Columbus, "Columbus went out not knowing where he was going; and when he got there he did not know where he was; and when he got back he did not know where he had been, and he did it all on other people's money."

This is the way of religion today. People do not know where they are, they do not know where they have been, they do not know why they are here, they do not know where they are going; and they do the whole thing on borrowed time, borrowed money, borrowed thinking, and then die. Science may be able to help keep you, but it cannot help you here. Science can keep you alive so that you have longer to think it over, but it will never give you any answer for the purpose of your life.

When I was 17 years old, I associated with a certain group of people. They were not educated people and certainly not scientists. They were plain, simple Christians, the saints and mystics, and the Brethren of the Common Life. They were the people of God and had a simple and more beautiful view of the world than many scientists. They did not know much, certainly not as much as a scientist, but they did know why they were here and where they were going. They celebrated their purpose of life by worshiping God enthusiastically and unashamedly.

Suppose I would visit some university and encounter a celebrated doctor of philosophy. I would not know nearly as much as he would know. However, if I met him downtown, wandering around, and he did not know where he was, I would know more than he would on that one thing.

He might stop me and ask, in a very cultured manner, "Where am I?"

I could say to him, "You're between Hamilton and Vineland."

"Thank you," he would say. I would smile to myself and think, *I have not studied in Germany, and I do not have all his degrees, but I know more than he did about one thing. I knew where he was, and he did not.*

I have read Albert Einstein's work on the fourth dimension and have never been able to understand it. I quit trying, but I take pleasure in knowing something Einstein did not know. I know why I am here. I belong to that company of plain Christians who believe a book called the Bible that says, "In the beginning God created the heaven and the earth" (Gen. 1:1).

God made man in His own image and blew in him the breath of life to live in His presence and worship Him. God then sent man out into the world to increase, multiply and fill the earth with men and women who would worship God in the beauty of holiness. That is our supreme purpose.

I do not walk around with my head down, looking sad, because somebody has written more books than I have or knows more than I know or has been to school longer than I have. Because I have a little secret: I can tell you why I was born, why I am here and my everlasting duties while the ages roll.

The plain people I admire so much say that God created the flowers to bloom so that man might enjoy them. God created the birds to sing for man's pleasure. However, no scientist would be caught dead admitting something that simple. The scientist has to come up with some complicated reasons of what this all means. The problem is, he never begins with God.

The scientist would object and say, "God did not create the birds to sing. Only the male bird sings, and he only sings to attract a female so he can have a nest of little ones. That is just simply a biological fact, that is all."

I think to myself, *Why couldn't the bird just warble or something? Why does the bird have to sing like a harp? Why do these birds sing so beautifully?* Because the God who made them is the composer of the cosmos. He made them, put a harp in their little throats, surrounded them with feathers and said, "Now, go sing." And they have been singing ever since, much to my delight.

I believe God that made the trees to bear fruit; but the scientist shrugs his shoulders and objects, "There you go again, you Christians. What a hopeless bunch you are. The trees bear fruit not for you but so there are seeds so that there will be more fruit."

God made the fruit, blessed it and told us to help ourselves. God also made the beast of the field to clothe mankind and the sheep to give us wool so that we can make a nice sweater to keep us warm in the winter. God made the humble little Japanese silk worm in the mulberry trees in order that we might spin their cocoon and make silk.

Throughout the Bible, the prophets and apostles all testify that God made us for a purpose and, according to them, that purpose is to sing His praises before the hushed audience of all creation. God created the silkworm to make silk; the bird was created to sing; the sheep for their wool. Everything in God's creation has its purpose.

Looking at the man He created, God said, "I am making man in my image and man is to be above all other creatures." Man's supreme purpose is to be above the beast of the earth and the birds of the air and the fish of the sea, even above the angels in the heaven. Ultimately, this man is to enter God's presence and unashamedly worship God, looking upon his face while the ages roll. That is why man was created; that is man's chief end.

Apart from that, we have no more idea why we are here. God gave you a harp and placed it in your own heart. God made you in order that you might stand up and charm the rest of the universe as you sing praises to the Lord Jesus Christ. That is why we were made in His image.

With Isaac Watts we can sing:

I'll praise my Maker while I've breath,
And when my voice is lost in death,
Praise shall employ my nobler powers.
My days of praise shall ne'er be past,
While life, and thought, and being last,
Or immortality endures.

Prayer

Lord God, for years we have wandered in the state of spiritual amnesia not knowing who we are, where we came from or what our purpose in life is. We knew not that we were made in Thy image for the single purpose of worshiping and adoring Thee. Our plight has been empty and futile. Then Christ, through the work of the Holy Spirit, awakened us to our true purpose in life. Now our days are filled with praise. And we praise Thee with our whole being, honoring Thee, adoring Thee in the beauty of Thy Holiness. Amen.

Searching for Man's Lost Identity

*Thou art worthy, O Lord, to receive glory and honour
and power: for thou hast created all things, and for thy
pleasure they are and were created.*

REVELATION 4:11

Christian ministry is based on the assumption that there are
some serious-minded people who want to know who they are,
what they are, why they are here and where they are going. Maybe
not many compared to the great masses of the world's popula-
tion, but enough to form a nice congregation almost everywhere you go. If I am wrong about this, I might as well leave my
Bible closed.

Searching for Purpose

But I firmly believe there are some who are serious and want to
know the answer to the question, "What is my purpose in life?"
Unfortunately, the masses have been given the wrong answer,
leading them farther away from the knowledge of God. This in-
cludes all the religions and philosophies of our world. This has
been a neat and successful trick of the enemy of man's soul.

Many people have tried to answer that question and consequently have led many people astray. Let me take several of them now and point out how empty and futile they really are; and may God deliver us from such utter foolishness.

Identity Through Work

Some would insist that our chief purpose in life is to work. No other place in the world, since the days of Adam to this present time, has given more honor to work than on the North American continent. Not that we like to work, we just like to talk about what an honorable thing it is.

Have you ever stopped to consider what work is?

Let me put work in its simplest form. Work is moving things and rearranging them. We have something over here and we work to put it over there. Something is in the pail and we put it on the side of the house, which we call painting. Something is in the cupboard, we work to put that into a skillet and then on the table to put it into your husband, and that is called cooking.

Smile at this simplification, but you will find this definition of work a very good and sound one. Work is taking something that is somewhere, putting it somewhere else and rearranging it. To the observer of humanity, the obvious thing about work is the fact that it has a short-range focus; it never has long-range purpose.

The farmer has some corn in his barn, puts it in the field and covers it up. After nature has worked on it for three or four months, he takes it from there and puts it back where he got it, only there is more of it. The next year the corn is gone;

the cattle ate the corn. Therefore, work always has a short-range purpose.

But what is the result of all this? Why do all this? Why put that green, red or white paint in that pail and put it on your house? You say, in order that the house might not be affected by the weather, that it might stay nice and look nice.

That is very good, but there never was a house built yet but it will rot and get rundown and finally be replaced with something newer. Nobody can convince me that I am merely made to work like a farm horse without having any future or any reason except that work. A man can work all his life, be identified by that work and then retire. Shortly after retirement, he dies because he has lost his purpose in life. The end result of work is utter futility.

Identity Through Education

Somebody else insists that we are here for a higher purpose than merely work. Our purpose is to educate ourselves, develop ourselves and perfect our intellectual nature. The process of this cultivation of the human mind is extensive.

A young person will go through school and be taught all the important things of life. He then might continue through college and learn science, art, literature and history. If he is ambitious, he will go on to do postgraduate work and get a degree.

I only see one little catch in this scenario. That young man, educated and well cultivated, is going to die and take all that education with him down into the grave. All that culture, that love of Bach, of Brahms and everything else will go right down with him into the grave.

Everything we do for a man is going to go right down into the grave with him when he dies. If he earns 40 degrees, they can put that on his tombstone, but he does not know anything about it. He is dead. Education alone is not the reason we were born. Our purpose is not for the perfecting of our intellectual nature, the education or development of our mind. I am not against education, because the alternative is simple ignorance. Education, however, does not answer the eternal purpose of why I am here.

Identity Through Pleasure

Others have a simpler viewpoint and tell us that we are here merely to enjoy ourselves. Epicurus, the father of Epicurean-ism, taught that pleasure is the chief end of man. Unfortunately, he earned a terrible reputation, but his idea was not as bad as it sounds. Epicurus did not teach that our purpose was to go out on a three-week binge or smoke opium or engage every physical and carnal pleasure known to man. He taught something quite the contrary.

Epicurus taught that pleasure is the end of all things: the pleasures of friendship and the beauty of literature and poetry and music and art. "The noble pleasures of a good conscience," he said, "is what we were born for in order that we might en-joy life."

Although he had good intentions and tried taking the high road, he had it all wrong. Joys and pleasures all pass away.

An old man who used to sit and listen enraptured to the music of the classics, now sits and nods in the corner and does not know Brahms from Frank Sinatra, because his mind is gone and his ability to enjoy pleasures is gone as well. What does a man do when life offers him no more pleasure? Some have answered this emptiness by suicide, a tragic end of a life that never found the real purpose of existence.

Identity Through Thrills

The younger and more energetic among us have the idea that the thrills of life are all that matter. Experiencing all the thrills of life is the ultimate point of living. It is a philosophy and is widely practiced and held by a good number of people who are not Christians. It is the philosophy that sex, food, sports, excitement and the gathering of goods is the chief end of man and our purpose in life. Our purpose in life is whatever produces a thrill.

Those who dedicate their time and the purpose of their life to getting a thrill out of life are going to have one of two things happen to them. Either they are going to run down physically or they are going to run down mentally until they lose all ability to experience any thrill anymore.

Nothing is quite as pathetic as an old rogue who has no thrill left anymore. A bored, weary, defeated, burned-out old man who has spent his life seeking physical thrills wherever he could find them and at any cost now is old, tired and burned out. Nothing thrills him anymore. Trying to get through to him is like sticking an ice pick into a wooden leg. There is no response, no reaction, no life or feeling left.

If that is all life is for, I think God made a terrible mistake when he created this whole world. If that is all, with my hand over my face, I cry to God Almighty, complain and say, "Why did You make me thus?"

Restored Identity

But, the exciting news is, that is not the reason or purpose of our life. I bring you to the Scriptures themselves, not to man's philosophy but to what God says about our purpose in life. The Scripture teaches us a number of things about the purpose of our life. It teaches us that God created all things out of His own pleasure. "Thou art worthy, O Lord, to receive glory and honour and power: for thou hast created all things, and for thy pleasure they are and were created" (Rev. 4:11).

When God decided to create mankind, it was a high day in heaven accompanied with a big celebration "when the morning stars sang together, and all the sons of God shouted for joy" (Job 38:7). Here was the heavenly host celebrating when God decided to create the heaven and the earth and, in particular, man to worship Him.

This is taught throughout the entire Bible, that God created man to worship Him. Man is the darling of the universe, the centerpiece of God's affection; however, many unbelievers denied this.

A very intelligent man once commented when asked what he thought to be the biggest mistake or error made by people: "I consider the biggest mistake to be the belief that we are special objects of Almighty God and that we are more than other things in the world, and God has a special fondness for people."

Regardless of that man's opinion, I base my whole life on the belief of God creating man with a special, unique, divine purpose. I do not care how brilliant this man is, he cannot jar me from my conviction. It would be as useless as throwing cooked peas at a 10-story building to destroy any of my beliefs or doctrines or commitment to this faith.

When a little baby is born into the world, the father searches intensely to see if the baby looks like him. He may be too tough to say it, but every father looks earnestly into the little wrinkled face to see whether it looks like him or not. We want things to look like us, and if they are not born to us, we go out and make them. We paint pictures; we write music; we do something, because we want to create. Everything we create is a reflection of our personality. In the world of art, a Monet is easily distinguished from a Rembrandt. Each painting reflects the personality of the artist.

God made man to be like Him so that man could give more pleasure to God than all the other creatures. Only in man, as created by God, can God admire Himself. Man is the mirror image in which God looks to see Himself. Man is the reflection of the glory of God, which was the purpose and intention of God originally. Man's supreme function through all eternity is to reflect God's highest glory, and that God might look into the mirror called man and see His own glory shining there. Through man, God could reflect His glory to all creation.

You are a mirror of the Almighty, and this is the reason you were created in the first place. This is your purpose. You are not created so that you might only take something over here and put it over there—*work*. You were not created only that you might develop your brain so that you can speak with a cultured accent—*education*. Neither are we here to enjoy ourselves, even the pure *pleasures* of life. Nor are we here for the *thrills* life brings.

All the holy prophets and apostles teach that man fell from his first estate and destroyed the glory of God, and the mirror was broken. God could no longer look at sinful man and see

His glory reflected. Man failed to fulfill the created purpose of worship to his Creator in the beauty of holiness. He forgot this, forfeited it by sin and is busy now finding other things to fill that emptiness. It is terrible what people will look to if they lose God. If there is no God in their eyes, then they get something else in their eyes; and if they do not enjoy worshiping the great God Almighty that made them, they find something else to worship.

If a person does not have God, he has to have something else. Maybe it is boats, or maybe it is money, amounting to idolatry, or going to parties or just simply raising the devil. They have lost God, and they do not know what to do, so they find something to do, which is why all the pleasures in life have been invented.

God made man to reflect His glory; but unfortunately, man does not. The flowers are still as beautiful as God meant them to be. The sun still shines yonder with spacious firmament on high. Evening shadows fall and the moon takes up the wonders and tells us whether the hand that made us is divine. Bees still gather their honey from flower to flower, and the birds sing a thousand songs and the seraphim still chant "holy, holy, holy" before the throne of God. Yet man alone sulks in his cave. Man, made more like God than any creature, has become less like God than any creature.

Man, made to be a mirror—to reflect the deity—now reflects only his own sinfulness. Sulking in his cave while the silent stars tell their story, man, except for his swearing, boasting, threatening, cursing and all the nervous and ill-conceived laughter and songs without joy, is silent before the universe.

Change the figure now from a mirror to a harp. God has put in man a harp bigger than anything else, and He meant that harp to be tuned to Himself. However, when man sinned and fell in this tragic and terrible thing we call the Fall of man, man threw that harp down into the mud; it is full of silt and sand, and the strings are broken.

The mightiest disaster ever known in the world was the soul of man, more like God than anything, and more fitted to God's sweet music than all other creatures, with the light gone from his mind and the love gone from his heart, stumbling through a dark world to find himself a grave. From God's point of view, man needed redemption. What is the purpose of redemption? Redemption is to restore us back to God again; to restring that harp; to purge it, cleanse it and refurbish it by the grace of God and the blood of the Lamb.

I have wonderful news for you. God, who made us like that, did not give up on us. He did not say to the angels, "Write them off and block them from my memory." Rather, He said, "I still want that mirror to shine in which I can look and see My glory. I still want to be admired in My people; I still want a people to enjoy Me and to love Me forever." Out of this insatiable passion, God sent His only begotten Son, and He became incarnated in the form of a man; and when He walked the earth, He was the reflected glory of God. God, finally, had His man.

The New Testament says, "Who being the brightness of his glory, and the express image of his person . . ." (Heb. 1:3). When God looked at Mary's son, He saw Himself reflected. Jesus said, "Believe me that I am in the Father, and the Father in me: or else believe me for the very works' sake" (John 14:11).

What did Jesus mean, "When you see me, you see the Father's glory reflected"? "I have glorified thee on the earth," said Jesus. "I have finished the work thou gavest Me to do," and there God glorified Himself in His son, and that Son went out to die, and all that glory was marred more than any man, and His features more than the son of man. They pulled out His beard, bruised His face, tore out His hair and made lumps on His forehead. Then they nailed Him on that cross where for six hours He sweated, twisted and groaned and finally gave up the ghost. The bells rang in heaven because man had been redeemed now. On the third day, He arose from the dead and now He is at God's right hand, and God now is busy redeeming the people back to Him again, back to the original purpose, to be mirrors reflecting God's glory.

I hope to explain what worship is and point out how tragically low this worship is among the churches. I hope to define worship and explain how we can recapture this worship for our generation and the generations to come.

Worship is man's full reason for existence. Worship is why we are born and why we are born again. Worship is the reason for our genesis in the first place and our regenesis that we call regeneration. Worship is why there is church, the assembly of the Redeemed, in the first place. Every Christian church in every country across the world in every generation exists to worship God first, not second; not tacking worship at the end of our service as an afterthought, but rather to worship God primarily, with everything else coming in second, at best. Worshiping God is our first call.

John Keats wrote of a tongueless nightingale ("The Eve of St. Agnes"). "As though a tongueless nightingale should swell Her throat in vain, and die, heart-stifled, in her dell." I have often thought that this great figure of speech was a beautiful thing. The tongueless nightingale died of suffocation because it had so much song in it that it could not get it out. We are the other way around. We have such a tremendous tongue and such little use for it. We have a harp such as no other creature in God's universe, but we play it so infrequently and so poorly.

When the saintly Brother Lawrence was dying, somebody asked him what he was doing. Without hesitation Brother Lawrence simply said, "I'm just doing what I've been doing for 40 years and expect to be doing throughout eternity."

"What's that?" the person inquired.

"Worshiping God."

As far as Brother Lawrence was concerned, dying was secondary, just an item on his agenda. His occupation was worshiping God above and before all other things. He had been worshiping God for 40 years, and facing death did not change that. When he felt his thoughts getting low, he was still worshiping God. He died, and they buried his body somewhere, but Brother Lawrence is still worshiping God in that coveted place we call the Presence of God.

You will be worshiping God long after everything else has ceased to exist. Too bad if you do not learn to worship Him now so that you do not have to cram for the last examination. For my part, I want to worship God in my own private life so fully and satisfyingly to the end so that I will not have to cram for the final exams. I can nearly stop breathing with quietness and say, "I worship Him; I am still worshiping Him; and I expect to worship Him for all eternity."

That is what you are here for, to glorify God and enjoy Him thoroughly and forever, telling the universe how great God is.

The Way of Perfection
by Frederick William Faber (1814-1863)

Oh how the thought of God attracts
And draws the heart from earth,
And sickens it of passing shows
And dissipating mirth!

'Tis not enough to save our souls,
To shun the eternal firs;
The thought of God will rouse the heart
To more sublime desires.

God only is the creature's home,
Though rough and straight the road;
Yet nothing less can satisfy
The love that longs for God.

Prayer

Oh, Thou God of the universe! The God that created all things that are, and created them for Thy pleasure, I humbly acknowledge Thee as my Creator. Restore to me the joy of Thy salvation. Restore the harp within that has been broken. Restring that harp in order that I might sing Thy praises throughout the universe and unto all the angels populating Thy heavens. In Jesus' name, amen.

Discovering the Heart of Man's Nature

So shall the king greatly desire thy beauty: for he is thy Lord;
and worship thou him.

PSALM 45:11

To the diligent student, the Bible is amazing in its consistency. The whole import and substance of the Bible is unswerving in what it teaches: that God created man to worship Him. That God, who does not need anything and who is complete in Himself, nevertheless desires worshipers. God in His uncreated nature is self-sufficient and possesses no lack whatsoever, yet He looks to man created in His image for worship. This represents a spiritual oxymoron. The Creator needs the creature.

This is the truth upon which I want to build; that God made everything for a purpose. His supreme purpose in making man was to have somebody capable to properly and sufficiently worship Him and satisfy His own heart. Man fell by sin and now is failing to carry out that created purpose. He is like

49

a cloud without water; it gives no rain. Like a sun that gives no heat or a star that gives no light or a tree that no longer yields fruit, a bird that no longer sings or a harp that is silent and no longer gives off music.

This is the longing of God's heart; deep calling unto deep. The Bible insists that when our Lord shall come, He shall be admired; He shall be glorified first in the saints and admired in all who believe. There is glorification and admiration, and our Lord is coming for that. "When he shall come to be glorified in his saints, and to be admired in all them that believe (because our testimony among you was believed) in that day" (2 Thess. 1:10).

The devil would like to tell us, for our own unbelieving minds, that God does not particularly desire our worship, as we owe it to Him. Satan would have us believe that God is not concerned or interested in our worship. But the truth is quite the contrary. God wants man to worship Him, and only redeemed man can worship Him acceptably. We are not unwanted children; God greatly desires our fellowship.

Why else would it be when Adam sinned and broke his fellowship with God that God came in the cool of the day, and when He could not find Adam called out, "Adam, where art thou?" It was God seeking worship from Adam who had sinned and in rebellion broke his fellowship. The harp within Adam had become unstrung and the voice of Adam choked in his throat.

God has commanded us to worship Him; and if you notice in Psalm 45:11, "So shall the king greatly desire thy beauty," God finds something in us that He put there for His personal pleasure. That "beauty" belongs to God.

This is quite contrary to what is usually heard in the average evangelical pulpit. Not only does God want man to worship Him, but man, even in his fallen state, has something within trying to respond, but not succeeding. Usually, we are told that men do not want to worship God. However, there is not a tribe in the world but practices some kind of religion and form of worship. The apostle Paul talked about the whole world stretching out its hands if perchance they might feel after God, so men desire to worship God.

Hymn writer Isaac Watts (1674-1748) expressed this for us in marvelous language:

Eternal Power
Eternal Power, Whose high abode
Becomes the grandeur of a God,
Infinite lengths beyond the bounds
Where stars resolve their little rounds!
The lowest step around Thy seat,
Rises too high for Gabriel's feet;
In vain the favored angel tries
To reach Thine height with wond'ring eyes.
There while the first archangel sings,
He hides his face behind his wings,
And ranks of shining thrones around
Fall worshiping, and spread the ground.
Lord, what shall earth and ashes do?
We would adore our Maker, too;
From sin and dust to Thee we cry,
The Great, the Holy, and the High.

Earth from afar has heard Thy fame,
And worms have learned to lisp Thy Name;
But, O! the glories of Thy mind
Leave all our soaring thoughts behind.
God is in Heaven, and men below;
Be short our tunes, our words be few;
A solemn reverence checks our songs,
And praise sits silent on our tongues.

When a man falls on his knees and stretches his hands heavenward, he is doing the most natural thing in the world. Something deep within compels him to seek someone or something outside of himself to worship and adore. In his unredeemed condition, man has lost the way and cannot clearly define the object of his wistful adoration, and so his search takes him far from God. When he does not find God, man will fill the void in his heart with anything he can find. That which is not God can never satiate the heart exclusively created for God's presence.

There is another facet of faith for our consideration. That is, we do not believe we are as dear to God as He says we are. We do not believe we are as precious or that He desires us as much as He says He does. The enemy of man's soul has sold this lie to us to not only beat us down, but to also keep us from the loving fellowship of God's presence. He cares not a whit for us, but his hatred of God drives him to do all in his power to deny God that which rightfully belongs to Him. If everybody could suddenly have a baptism of pure cheerful belief that God wants and desires us to worship, admire and praise Him, it could transform us overnight into the most radiantly happy people in the world. We would finally discover our purpose: that God delights in us, and longs for our fellowship.

If man had not fallen, worship would continue to be the most natural thing because God specifically designed man to worship Him. God created man as His special instrument of music—offering to Him natural sweet praise. However, when man rebelled and fell away from this purpose, when sin came into his life, sin has become natural. Man's nature is fallen, but this was not God's original intention for us. If everybody had cancer, then we could say cancer was natural and accept it as so. However, it is not natural, because when God made the human body, He did not have in mind wild cells forming called cancer and destroying man.

When God made the human soul in His own image, He did so that we might act according to that Divine nature. He never intended the virus of sin to infect that sacred place within man. Sin, therefore, is the unnatural thing. It is a foreign substance defiling man's heart and life, repelling God's gaze. Because of this condition in man, sin is natural, worship is unnatural; and so few people really do it.

Because of this, it is important to understand that nobody can devise their own pattern of worship or worship God any way they please. The pleasure here belongs to God alone. The One who created us to worship Him also has decreed how we shall worship Him. We cannot worship God as we will; our worship must always conform to God's pleasure. God does not accept just any kind of worship. He accepts worship only when it is pure and when it flows from a heart under the afflatus of the

Holy Spirit. Only such worship, compatible with His holy nature, can possibly be accepted by Him.

This deception destroys the lives of multitudes of people in every generation. It is a favorite ploy of the devil and a favorite pet of unconverted poets to suggest that we just worship God any way we want to worship and at our whim, and all will be well, as long as we are sincere.

The fallacy in this is the fact that religious experience is altogether possible apart from Christ and apart from redemption. It is entirely feasible to have an authentic religious experience and not be a Christian and to be on your way to an eternal hell. It happens all the time all over the world.

It might be hard to conceive, but it is entirely possible to have an experience with God and yet not have a saving experience with God. So not only is it possible to have a religious experience apart from Christ, and apart from salvation, but it is also possible to have worship apart from Christ and apart from salvation. This is chilling to think it is possible to go through the motions of worship and not worship right. "They worshiped they know not what," said Jesus of a certain group. It is possible to have elements of worship: adoration, self-abasement, surrender and man still not be redeemed at all.

Thomas Carlyle in his "Heroes and Hero Worship" warned us not to make the mistake of thinking that the great pagan religions of the world were all counterfeit. He said, "It's not true they were phony, they were real and the terror of them was that they were real."

I once visited an old church in Mexico with a dirt floor. I walked in and took off my hat and observed all the statues and candles. While there, I saw an old Mexican woman come in and walk straight down to the front as if she knew the way and could go in the dark with her eyes closed; she had been there so often. She walked straight to a statue, I think it was the Virgin, knelt and looked up into the face of that statue with a longing and devotion that I would like to see turned to the Lord Himself. She was having an experience of worship, and it was real to her. She was no phony, she was a real worshiper; but look what she was worshiping. Her worship was not directed in the right direction. The sad part about this whole thing is that she did not know it.

The American Indian would stand on the bank of the river, stretch his red arms up to the sky and say to the Manito, "Praises be, praises be to the Manito, praises be." He was experiencing real worship when he cried to his Great Manito.

It is entirely possible to have a religious experience without God, and even reject the God of the Bible. It is possible to have an experience of worship, but not according to the will of God and, consequently, unacceptable with God, because God hates idolatry. Idolatry is simply worship directed in any direction but God's, which is the epitome of blasphemy.

The apostle Paul understood this: "But I say, that the things which the Gentiles sacrifice, they sacrifice to devils, and not to God: and I would not that ye should have fellowship with devils. Ye cannot drink the cup of the Lord, and the cup of devils: ye cannot be partakers of the Lord's table, and of the table of devils" (1 Cor. 10:20-21).

Our Lord said that there would be a day when people would say, "Lord, Lord, have we not prophesied in thy name? and in thy name have cast out devils? and in thy name done many wonderful works? And then will I profess unto them, I never knew you: depart from me, ye that work iniquity" (Matt. 7:22-23). He did not accept their worship. He could not accept their worship because it was not according to the holy nature of God. God cannot accept any worship apart from Himself and incompatible with His holiness.

The One who made us to worship Him also has decreed how we should go about the worship of Him. We cannot worship God as we will, according to our pleasure or mood. God does not accept just any kind of worship. He accepts worship only when it is pure and directed by the Holy Spirit. God has rejected almost all the worship of humanity in our present condition. However, God wants us to worship Him, commands us to and asks us to. Obviously, He was anxious and hurt when Adam failed to worship Him. Nevertheless, God condemns and rejects almost all the worship of humanity.

A worshiper must submit to God's truth or he cannot worship God. He can write poems and get elevations of thought when he sees a sunrise. But he cannot worship God except in faith and according to God's revealed truth. To worship as God can accept means submitting to the truth about God, admitting who God says He is and to admit that Christ is who and what He says He is.

Furthermore, he has to admit the truth about himself that he is as bad a sinner as God says he is. This is the last barrier to repentance. Man in his lost condition refuses to own up to his sinfulness. "God made me this way," so he boasts to alleviate any personal guilt. If I am not responsible for my condition,

I do not need to make any changes. God has to accept me as I am.

Then, he has to admit to the truth of the atonement, the blood of Jesus Christ that cleanses and delivers us from sin, and come God's way. When someone finally owns up to his sinful condition, he is often tempted to make his own atonement. But this has a major flaw. It does not meet God's standard.

For worship to be acceptable to God, you must be renewed after the image of Him that created you. That "image" must be restored. Only the renewed man can worship God in a way worthy of and acceptable to Him.

If the Holy Spirit does not do these things, it would only be wood, hay and stubble. My worship will never reach higher than the top of my own head, and God in heaven will refuse it as He refused the worship of Cain. I have a book, the Bible, which enlightened me. Here is the "light that lighteth every man" that will read it. Jesus Christ is the "light that lighteth every man that cometh into the world." The light of the human heart and the light of this book harmonize; and when the eyes of the soul look to the living Word of God, then we know the truth and we can worship God with truth and in spirit.

In the Old Testament, a priest could not offer a sacrifice until he had been anointed with oil, symbolic of the Spirit of God. No man can worship out of his own heart. Let him search among the flowers, let him search among the bird nests and tombs and wherever he chooses to worship God. Such a search will be futile and lead to spiritual frustration.

He cannot worship out of his own heart. Only the Holy Spirit can worship God acceptably, and He must in us reflect back to God His own glory. If it does not reach our hearts, there is no reflecting back and no worship.

O how big and broad and comprehensive and wonderful is the work of Christ! That is why I cannot have too much sympathy for the kind of Christianity that makes out that the gospel is to save a person from smoking or drinking. Is that all Christianity does, keep me from some bad habit, so I will not play the ponies, beat my wife or lie to my mother-in-law? Of course, regeneration will clean that up, and the new birth will make a man right. Those are the effects of a nature redeemed by the blood of Christ.

The primary purpose of God in redemption is to restore us again to the divine imperative of worship so that we can hear God say again, "So shall the king greatly desire thy beauty: for he is thy Lord; and worship thou him" (Ps. 45:11). The Church Militant conquered the world with their joyous religion because and only because they were worshipers. When the Christian church in any generation ceases to be a company of worshipers, their religion succumbs to mere outer effects, empty works and meaningless rituals.

When you begin to talk about the Lamb that was slain, and the blood that was shed, and God the Father, God the Son and God the Holy Ghost, then you are living and worshiping in truth. When the Spirit of God takes over, we worship in spirit and in truth; and that worship exceeds mere external rituals.

God created you to worship Him. When fundamentalism lost her power to worship, she invented religious claptrap to make her happy. That is why I have hated it, preached against it, condemned it all these years. Claiming to serve the Lord, the only joy they have is the joy that is of the flesh. Elvis Presley was a happier man after he got through with his sensuous music than many Christians are after they have worked themselves up in an emotional frenzy for half an hour.

For the redeemed, the well of the Holy Spirit is an effervescing artesian well, and you do not have to prime the pump. The silver waters of the Holy Spirit flooding up and out of the redeemed and cleansed heart of a worshiping man are as sweet and beautiful to God as the loveliest diamond. We need to learn how to worship to please the God who deserves it.

"So shall the king greatly desire thy beauty: for he is thy Lord; and worship thou him."

Prayer

God our Father, we seek Thee in ways that will bring us to Thee. We turn to the Holy Spirit, to our guide and teacher. May our hearts yield to His work and may He so flood our hearts with joy unspeakable and full of glory that we rise above the din of the world into the Light Unapproachable.

THE VARIOUS PATHS TO WORSHIP

My heart was hot within me, while I was musing the fire burned:
then spake I with my tongue.

PSALM 39:3

Deep within every human is the impulse to worship, and it is the most natural thing about us. Not all paths, however, lead to the worship God accepts and delights in. Certain kinds of worship are abhorrent to God and He cannot accept it, even though it is directed toward Him and is meant to be given to Him. The God who desires worship insists the worship be on His terms, and He allows no exception.

In every generation and culture, there have been primarily four pathways men and women have taken in their pursuit of worship. Let me name them for you. These four categories are true in every generation and culture and have withstood the passing of time.

The Path of Human Excellence

This path to worship comes so close but falls so far short of God's requirement. This worship is beautiful in many regards and represents man's effort at his best. It is giving God what we delight in, disregarding God's command.

The Old Testament is a beautiful illustration of this in the life of Cain. Abel offered unto God the sacrifice of blood while Cain offered a sacrifice without blood. Abel brought to God according to His delight, while Cain brought to God what delighted him without any regard to God. God condemned and rejected the worship of Cain, because it lacked atonement.

Cain came to worship without a blood sacrifice, which is atonement; he came to God with a gift of his choosing for his Creator. He plucked a nice bunch of flowers and some nice delicious fruit and took it to God. God inquired after the blood and Cain said, "What blood?" Cain did not understand that he could not come to God without blood atonement. Cain objected, "I don't care about sin, I'll just bring a gift." He came before God with a bloodless sacrifice and offered flowers and fruit and the growth of the earth to the Lord.

This path of human excellence is not acceptable to God for a variety of reasons. Its basic premise is that God is unnecessary and that by human effort and devotion, we can reach the standard God wants for us. This kind of worship rests upon a mistaken assumption regarding the nature of God. Cain was born of Adam and Eve, fallen parents, and had never heard the voice of God in the Garden himself. When Cain came to worship God, he came to a God of his own imagination, thinking he was acceptable to God in his present condition.

Abel, on the other hand, brought a lamb, and God accepted it. When God refused Cain's worship it infuriated him, and he went out and in a jealous rage committed the first murder. Cain did not comprehend the difference God made between the two offerings. He took it upon himself to assume what would please God and completely disregarded the nature of God.

This kind of worship is all about us even today, even within the confines of what is called the Christian Church. A man can be well educated and even graduate from a seminary and can be taught how to use hand gestures and how to open his mouth and sound learned. He can be a ready-made preacher with all the culture the world of religion can offer. But if he follows the path of human excellence to worship, no matter how beautiful it might be, it will not be acceptable in God's eyes.

Worship acceptable to God is based upon knowing the nature of God. Cain did not know the kind of God he was, and therefore thought that sin was nothing to God. This represented a gross misunderstanding of God's nature.

This path to worship assumes a relationship to God that does not exist. Cain believed he belonged to God and assumed that he could talk to God without an intermediary. Cain failed to understand that he was alienated from God by his sin. Therefore, he never dealt with this sin element that was separating him from God. He acted as though there was no such separation and ignored the implications of such a separation.

Many religious people mistakenly assume a relationship to God that does not exist. They think and teach that we are all God's children, and they talk about the God and Father of mankind. However, the Bible does not teach that God is the Father of mankind; in fact, it teaches the exact opposite. To assume a relationship that does not exist prohibits a person from really knowing God.

Another thing about the path of human excellence is in the area of sin. For example, Cain viewed sin as being less severe than God viewed it. Sin is dismissed as inconsequential to our worship of God. Sin, however, is serious, and God never smiles upon it and never looks at any heart with sin upon it. He hates sin because it has filled the world with pain and sorrow but, more importantly, because it has robbed man of his purpose in life of worshiping God.

Cain represents the excellence of human accomplishment in this area of worship. He thought God was a different kind of God from what He is. He thought he was a different kind of man than what he was and thought sin was less vicious and serious than God said it was. So he came cheerfully, bringing his best, and offered to God worship without atonement.

While God says, "He is thy Lord, worship thou Him," and while He calls "where art thou" and commands us to worship Him in "spirit and in truth," He bluntly and severely rejects worship not founded on redeeming blood.

Apart from the blood atonement on the cross, no church holds any attraction for me. Without the redemption by the blood of Jesus Christ, there is no salvation. This path to worship, no matter how gentle and tender it is or how it may be adorned with beautiful flowers plucked from all parts of the world, is still false, and God frowns upon it because it is false in itself. God simply rejects the path of human excellence to worship.

The Path of Heathen Darkness

If Cain represents man at his best, then heathen worship is man at his worst. Completely disregarding all dignity, man subjects himself to the basest elements of his nature and worships the creation instead of the Creator. It would take a five-foot shelf of books for me to write, even if I were able to do it, to put forth adequately the tenants of this. I could go back if I wanted to and search in to the worship of the early Egyptians, the Egyptian book of the dead and the writings of Zoroaster and Buddha. We could make a case and talk about the worship of the pagans.

Paul talks about this and does not have a kind thing to say about it. He condemns it outright and says, "Because that, when they knew God, they glorified him not as God, neither were thankful; but became vain in their imaginations, and their foolish heart was darkened" (Rom. 1:21).

Down they ascended from God to man and from man to bird and from bird to beast and from beast to fish and from fish to creeping things that wiggled on the earth. That was man's terrible trip downward in his worship. This is man trying his best to be his worst and succeeding beyond expectation. God rejects and completely disowns this kind of worship and any worshipers involved in it.

I believe that if the Christian Church has not crossed the line already, it is perilously close to slipping into heathen oriented worship, rendering to the creature what rightfully belongs to the Creator. Let me explain what I mean. Never has there been a time in Christian history where the Church has been more plagued with celebrities than today, especially in the music department.

On a Saturday night, a "praise and worship band" will hold a concert in a hall downtown. After one song, the audience explodes in applause accompanied with cheers and a standing ovation. To cover his track, the lead singer will say, "Let's give a clap offering to God."

If you do not think this is crowding the line, do this. Take the lyrics of the song that caused such uproar and give it to one of the dear old saints at church on Sunday. Make sure it is one of those saints with an impeccable reputation of holiness and unimpeachable Christian character. Usually this will be one of the saintly prayer warriors of the church. Have this person take these lyrics to the pulpit and quietly read them to the audience. If it does not create the same effect as the night before, maybe it was not the truth in those lyrics the people the night before were applauding but the performers.

The path of heathen darkness to worship always mirrors the culture around it rather than the Christ within.

The Path of Heretical Confusion

This is heretical worship in the correct meaning of the term. A heretic is not a man who denies all the truth; he is just a very fastidious man who picks out what he likes while rejecting what he does not like. Certain aspects of theology appeal to him, but others are rejected because they do not suit him at the time. I refer to these as inconvenient aspects of theology.

A man once addressed a large group of Christian young people offering this advice: "Don't believe anything in the Bible that doesn't square with your own experience." This man had the infinite effrontery to tell young people searching for truth to take the Word of God and judge it by their little wicked hearts. How can you get any worse than that? It is heretical confusion at its best. Heresy means I take what I like and I reject what I do not like. The very word "heretic" means one who picks and chooses. But the Bible says, "And if any man shall take away from the words of the book of this prophecy, God shall take away his part out of the book of life, and out of the holy city, and from the things which are written in this book" (Rev. 22:19).

The Samaritans of Jesus' day represented this kind of worship. The Samaritans were heretics in the right sense of the word, because being heretical does not always mean that we are false. A man can be a heretic and not teach anything particularly false. A heretic does not necessarily teach that there is no Trinity, or that God did not create the earth, or that there is no judgment. Heresy is the selecting and rejecting aspects of truth and applying psychology, humanism and the various religions of all sorts. Every religion is based upon this.

The Lord rejects this path to worship because of its selective nature, picking what it likes and what does not inconvenience its lifestyle. If it does not like something, it explains it away and goes on as if it were a small matter or if it even did not exist.

The Samaritans were heretics in that they chose certain parts of the Bible, the Old Testament. They had a Pentateuch and accepted it but rejected certain parts of David, Isaiah, Jeremiah, Ezekiel and Daniel, 1 and 2 Kings, the Song of Solomon and other parts of Scripture. They believed them and did some translating.

You can translate anything and prove anything. All a person has to say is, "I know Greek" or "I know Hebrew," and after that, that person is on his or her own. He or she is a self-appointed expert on the subject. Every false religion or cult is built on the selecting of favorite Scripture passages to the neglect of other passages. They do not compare Scripture with Scripture, which allows heretical doctrine to come in.

The Samaritans translated the old Pentateuch in such a way as to make Samaria the place of worship. And, of course, they were hostile to the Jews who insisted Jerusalem was the only place to worship Jehovah. The Samaritans used their translation of the Pentateuch to prove their position.

God gave Israel Mount Mariah, and here David took Zion and Solomon built the Temple, and that was the place where the people should worship. It was there Christ came and became the sacrificial Lamb for the sins of mankind. However, the Samaritans refused Jerusalem in favor of Samaria. They did so by selecting certain parts of the Pentateuch to support that position.

I do not think I will have to spell it out and mark it in red ink for you to see how much heresy there is these days. Believing what we want to believe. Emphasizing what we want to emphasize. Following along in one path while rejecting another. Doing one thing but refusing another. We become heretics by picking and choosing among the Word of God what suits us at the time. That is the path of heretical confusion.

The Path of Existential Sublimity

I admit that I have more sympathy with this category than I do with liberalism, which is the enemy of true biblical Christianity (of which Samaritan worship is one). At the same time, I reject this path to worship, which is but the poetry of religion. Religion does have a lot of poetry in it; it is proper, and it should have. Personally, I melt like honey on a hot day when I get to this existential. Poetry is the high enjoyment and contemplation of the sublime.

By nature, we are all poets, and religion brings poetry out more than any other occupation the mind can be engaged in. Moreover, there is a lot that is very beautiful about religion. You will discover a high enjoyment in the contemplation of the divine and sublime. The concentration of the mind upon beauty always brings a high sense of enjoyment.

Some mistake this sublimity, this rapt feeling for true worship, and it is an understandable mistake. God warned Israel that when they arrived in the Promised Land and looked up and saw the sun and the stars, they were not to get on their knees and worship them because if they did, Jehovah would destroy them from out of the land. The world is full of these worshipers. It is a high enjoyment, a concentrating of the mind upon beauty as distinct from the eye and the ear. If your ear hears beauty that is music, or your eye sees beauty that is art, but if you think beautiful thoughts without music or art, that is poetry. We write what we feel inside, and that is poetry.

Some people understandably mistake such rapturous feelings for worship. Ralph Waldo Emerson said, "I have crossed the meadow after a rain on a moonlight night when the moon had come out and the rain and the puddles were still lying in the meadow and the moon shining on the little puddles of water in the grass and I have been glad to the point of fear." He was so happy that he was afraid. I have felt it myself. Emerson did not believe in the deity of Christ or the blood of Christ, and he resigned his church rather than serve communion. He eventually denied the faith. Yet he was glad to the point of fear, because he was a good man. He was a great man, a poet and an artist. A mighty man indeed, but I do not think God accepted his worship at all because it led along the path of existential sublimity, and that was all.

It is easy to confuse the music of religion as true worship because music elevates the mind and raises the heart to near rapture. Music can lift our feelings to a sense of ecstasy. Music has a purifying effect upon us so that it is possible to fall into a happy and elevated state of mind with only a vague notion about God and imagine we are worshiping God when we are doing nothing of the sort. We are simply enjoying an ecstatic moment God put in us that even sin has not yet been able to kill.

I reject the idea of any poetry in hell; I cannot believe that among the terrible sewage of the moral world there is going to be anybody breaking into similes and metaphors. I cannot conceive of anyone breaking into song in that terrible place called hell. We read about music and poetry in heaven because it belongs there. As far as I know in my Bible, we never hear about poetry in hell. We hear about conversations in hell, but we do not hear about song because there is no song there. There is no poetry there, no music there, but plenty of it on earth, even among the unsaved because they were once made in the image of God. While they have lost God from their mind, they still appreciate the sublime and carry within their innermost part a residue of spiritual desire.

Certain men have written books on the importance of sublimity and how to cultivate it. And there is much that is inspirational and beautiful in the world. Sublimity is beauty of the mind in contradistinction (to use a long word), beauty of the eye and ear. Music is the beauty that the ear recognizes. And certain other beautiful things the eye recognizes, but when the heart hears nothing and sees nothing but only feels, then it is the music of the heart. It is beauty within the spirit.

The Scripture tells us that "God is a Spirit: and they that worship him must worship him in spirit and in truth" (John 4:24). The Word must clear away all the mists of obscurity. It takes worship out of the hands of men and puts it in the hands of the Holy Spirit. Therefore, we can have all that and still not worship God at all or even be accepted of God.

We may take whatever path to worship we choose, but not all paths will end at the feet of the Lord Jesus Christ, nor will God accept them. God Almighty sternly rejects it all and says, "I will have nothing to do with it." Jesus our Lord said, "God is Spirit: and they that worship him must . . ." I want you to see the imperative; the word "must" clears away all mists of obscurity and takes worship out of the hands of man.

It is impossible to worship God acceptably apart from the Holy Spirit. The operation of the Spirit of God within us enables us to worship God acceptably through that person we call Jesus Christ, who is Himself God. Therefore, worship originates with God, comes back to us and is reflected from us. That is the worship God accepts, and He accepts no other kind.

Prayer

Oh, God, we ask Thee that as we speak, heaven might be open and there might be a sense of Thy presence and the feeling that there is impending upon this world another world above, an eternal world touching Thee. As the kingdom of heaven touches the kingdom of man, we believe God has heard our prayers. Oh, God, we pray, speak Thou and let us not take anything for granted, let us not believe that something is true when it is not true or assume we are all right when we are not or think that our worship is acceptable when it is not. May we one and all, each and every one of us come humbly, looking to the sacrifice, the mighty sacrifice, and hear the words of love and see the mighty sacrifice and have peace with Thee. Grant this we pray in Christ's holy name. Amen.

The Fervor of Holy Desire
by Madame Guyon

Still, still, without ceasing.
I feel it increasing,
This fervor of holy desire;
And often exclaim,
Let me die in a flame that can never expire!

RELIGION VERSUS WORSHIP

*God is a Spirit: and they that worship him must
worship him in spirit and in truth.*

JOHN 4:24

Since man's expulsion from the Garden, religion has been an intolerable burden on the back of all mankind. In spite of the drudgery, it is a bondage most are unable or unwilling to break. The word "religion" itself means to bind back; religious people, as a rule, have laid off one set of chains only to take up another. Whatever it takes, man will exercise this inward impulse to worship.

Then along comes our Lord and issues a long-awaited spiritual emancipation proclamation and signs it in blood. Now the people of the world, bearing the heavy yoke of religion, can know the true freedom of genuine worship. Our Lord Jesus spoke words allowing the light to shine upon us so that there is light in our spirits, elevating us and lifting us up out of the mud of depraved society.

God never called man to walk knee-deep in the sludge of the world, nor did He intend for man to be mired down in the traditions of men. Therefore, the Lord sets us free and opens a fountain of healing water for the wounds of the world.

In spite of all this, man deliberately chooses the bondage of religion over the liberating freedom in Christ.

In India, they believe that the goddess Ganga that is the Ganges River has power to cleanse people. Certain saints make pilgrimages to bathe in goddess Ganga, one of the dirtiest rivers in the world. They will fall down full length and then mark with their finger where their forehead was, step forward and put their foot where the mark is and then fall full length again. Literally, they fall across scores of miles to the goddess Ganga, the River Ganges, and bathe themselves, go away and are no cleaner than they were before. In fact, they are not as clean as they were before. Certainly they are wounded and bruised bitterly in their soul.

Our Lord puts into one sentence the words of worship: "God is a Spirit: and they that worship him must worship him in spirit and in truth," forever settling this matter and emphasizing that you cannot please God by bruising your body or by bathing in this or that river. However, they that worship the Father worship Him in spirit and in truth. This is the true healing water for the wounded souls of religious men.

Our Lord explains here that worship is natural to man. There has never been a tribe of people discovered anywhere but what religion was a part of its society. It was perfectly natural for Adam to walk with God in the garden in the cool of the day. The years of Adam were blessed by the velvet-soft, healing voice of God. When Adam sinned, he hid from the presence of God among the trees of the garden. He was conscious of God, but he was not free to worship God, because sin had come in between and tore the strings off the harp. Nothing remained but the outline; the music of the soul was muted; now there was cacophony and discord where there had been harmony before. So he lost the proper object of his worship and was looking about now for something to worship.

Man worships by the necessity of his being. Looking around for something to worship, he recognizes mystery and wonder. The result is, whatever man cannot explain, he will worship. Whatever evokes wonder becomes the object of man's worship. Because the human mind is fallen, he is amazed at external things and objects that impress.

The human mind is enlarged, lifted and filled with wonder, and this very wonder leads to worship and opens mystery. Men used to stand on the seashore and hear the moaning of the sea and watch the gulls turn and see the white clouds float, and cry, "What is all of this, what is all of this?" And they called that something out there Neptune, and said, "This is our God," and got on their knees and made sacrifices to Neptune. The splendor of nature called to mind a need to worship not the Creator but the creation. When they saw the sun rising in the morning and making its journey across the sky, and setting in the sea of blood, they said, "What is this shining thing that always rises in the same place and goes down and never fails?" They called it Phoebus Apollo—a great beautiful god they made with silver wings on his feet so that he went fast across the sky. They worshiped and said this is wonderful. They did not know what it was, but it was wonderful and inspired a need to worship. The Parsis got on their knees before the sun; they called it Mazda, and the light that shines down is Mazda light named after the god of the Zoroastrians, the fire worshipers.

If we do not know how to worship through Jesus Christ our Lord, the human heart will break out somehow like a flood that goes over its banks and will worship. If it does not get going in the right direction, it will go in the wrong direction; but it will worship.

Not only in nature did man find reason to worship but also within the heart and emotions of man. They said, "Look at love, look at this powerful, tremendous thing for which men and women die and think nothing of it. Look at this that binds a man and woman together, binds family together, binds men to the love of their country until they will give and sacrifice themselves freely." They called it Venus; we have named one of the planets after that goddess. We could go on; there is Ceres, the goddess of life, and many others—the list is as endless as the imagination of man. Every emotion, every thought, every imagination of man became the object of mystery and adoration—all leading away from the One behind all this, the Creator.

Another indication of this need to worship can be seen in the artistic and creative work of man. What makes a man want to create something beautiful? Why does he want to write a poem, paint a picture, compose a piece of music? I believe that fallen man has within him somewhere, in the deep of his soul, that which calls out after mystery. Deep calls unto deep at the noise of God's waterspout; the deep voice of God calls and the deep of man struggles to answer back.

Every time a Greek got on his knees at the seashore and offered his sacrifice to Neptune, it was the little blind deep within him answering back to the deep of God. Every time an American Indian stood on the shore of the river and reverently put the bones of the fish back into the sea and apologized to God for killing it and eating it; every time he looked up and said "Manito," and "Praises be," he was giving up to the mystery within him. And every time that great genius Beethoven turned out a page of immortal music, he was feeling something deep within. He was saying, "I know God. He is nearer to me than He is to others; I know this God," and then he wrote his imperishable music. What was he doing? Flinging out wildly, looking to worship something, anything. This great man who hovered back and forth between suicide and life until he gave up and went the way of all flesh was only a sample.

Man has it in him to do this—to admire, to fear—and consequently, many religions have developed because of this. In India, there is a god for everyone, to answer to the compulsion within to worship. By nature man has to admire something. Within his very being he has to adore, and if he loses his ability to adore in his spirit and soar in his heart, he will find some other way to do it. He will get out there somehow. Because of how he was created, man is drawn to mystery wherever he finds it. Some mystery creates within a sense of awe, and when he finds it, he will worship.

This is the impulse behind exploring other worlds and riding out into the vast spaces in the heavens. No other of God's creatures do it, and no other creature thinks of doing it. Man, who has lost the mystery of God within his heart, looks for that mystery elsewhere.

The Samaritan woman in John 4 revealed what is wrong with the entire religious world: "Sir, I understand from what you say that you are a prophet. You know more than the average person would know; you must be a prophet. I've got a question for you." This question was not simply a frivolous one; it was one that separated Jew from Samaritan even though they were related by blood. The question was, "Here in Samaria, in our holy mountain, we worship. Across there a little way in Jerusalem the holy mountain of the Jews, they worship. And we say this is the place to worship and you say Jerusalem is the place to worship. Now, you are a prophet; tell me, where is the right place to worship?"

This woman falls into her own little trap and reveals that chief woe of the religious world. Do I worship here or do I worship there? Do I worship in this church or do I worship in that church? What church is the right church and what denomination is the right one? That is the difficulty and the problem. The whole problem then was externality of worship. Externalism is our problem even today—the biggest problem the church faces.

Jesus our Lord said this beautiful thing: "The time is fast approaching, in fact it is already here where worship won't be tied down to any location, for the Father seeketh such to worship Him in spirit for God is spirit and therefore you must be spiritual worshippers" (see John 4:21-23). If God were a local deity confined to a hill, you would have to go to the hill to worship Him. If God were a river deity confined to the river, you would have to go down to the bank of the river to worship Him. If God were a mountain deity, or if God were a plains deity, you would have to go where He was. Jesus gave us the marvelous liberating news that God is Spirit; therefore, God is everywhere, and we do not worship in places anymore.

The purpose of nature is to lead us to the Creator and to worship Him. The purpose of man's feelings and emotions is to lead to the One who implanted those within the heart of man, to the Creator. Everything in all of creation is to point to the Creator and evoke within adoring wonder and admiration and worship. Wherever we go, we can worship.

Jesus taught essentially that we are portable sanctuaries, and if we are worshiping in spirit and in truth, we can take our sanctuary around with us. Jesus said, "Don't you see that if God is Spirit, worship is spiritual, and anything spiritual has no location in space and it has no location in time?" You do not get up in the morning, look at your calendar and say this is the time to worship. You do not get up, go out, look around and say this is the place to worship. You worship God now, anywhere, any place, any time, because worship is spiritual.

People have made a comedy of religion, because men have enslaved themselves to externals and objects to the point of the ridiculous. These religious pilgrims travel to their holy shrines in order to worship. Many will take a pilgrimage to the Holy Land and believe they are closer to God there than anywhere else on the planet. In God's kingdom, as He has intended it, no place is holier than another. If you cannot worship here, you cannot worship there.

It does not stop here, this bondage of religion. Some make their religion to consist in foods. Some things they do not eat and some things they do eat. The result is that if they do eat it, they are holy; and if they do not eat it, they are not holy. At certain times of the year, you can eat "this," but not at other times of the year. Paul explained that what you ate did not make you better and it did not make you any worse. It might make you sick, but it will not make you holy and it will not hurt you nor help you. If it is decent and good, and you can digest it, help yourself. Holiness does not reside in the food we eat, and worship is not dependent upon that food either. God is a Spirit: and they that worship Him must worship Him in spirit and in truth.

Then, some are enslaved to times. Worship is not in times. I respect our brethren of the church calendar year that begins with one thing and ends with another; but I do not follow it at all. Can you imagine that six weeks out of the year I repent; then after that the lid is off? I could not imagine myself being tied down to times. "Behold now is the accepted time." This is the time; so any time is all right. You can say, "Good morning, God," in the morning. You can say, "Goodnight, God," at night. You can wake in the night and think of God; you can even dream of God—I have. You can have God any time, any place.

There are times of the year when we think of religion a little more. I personally like Easter. If I were going to have a special time of the year, it would be Easter, because that is when birds are returning from Florida and the people of God are looking up and we are hearing, "Christ the Lord Is Risen Today, Hallelujah, Hallelujah." I like Easter, and I think it is a beautiful time of the year. I have a tough time preaching Easter sermons because all of my sermons are based upon His resurrection; and if you take away the resurrection of Jesus Christ, my sermons collapse.

Christ's resurrection is not truer at Easter than any other time of the year. Apart from the resurrection of Christ, all of

Christianity falls to the ground. Our worship cannot be confined to time.

Foods are not holy; times are not holy; and places are not holy. If they do not point to Christ, they become a snare enslaving us to mere religious bondage.

The Jews made the mistake of thinking the Temple was holy; and because the Temple was holy, nothing could happen to the Temple. Jesus pointed out their error. "See this Temple? See these stones? Every bit of it will lie in the dust before very long." It came down to the ground in the year A.D. 70. He said Israel is like a tree. "See that ax, either it will bear fruit or it will be cast down into the fire."

I am talking about worship now and saying worship is a spiritual thing. It is internal; and external things are unnecessary. For instance, we could not sit on the street corner and preach, sing and pray. We need walls to protect us, or heat to keep us warm. Buildings have a place and purpose, so I am not against buildings. You have to have books, and I am for books. God has blessed external things, but the trouble is that we become slaves to them instead of making them our servants.

So, with times and foods and everything else, they are our servants. Therefore, we rise above all the little things of religion and look down on them from our place in the heavenlies. It is wonderful how small things look when you are up high enough. You always know that you are losing altitude when things begin to get big. When fields get the size of postage stamps, you are really up there. When they begin to get a little bit bigger, you are losing altitude; you look at your watch, and say, "We're going to land." The further down, the bigger things look; and the higher up, the smaller. I recommend to you concerning a big problem facing you, rise above it, take off and get up there above it.

True worship elevates us above all the accoutrements of religion into that rarified atmosphere of God's holy and delightful presence. Seventeenth-century French mystic Madame Guyon put these thoughts into a hymn we often sing in church.

Content
by Madame Guyon

My Lord, how full of sweet content,
I pass my years of banishment!
Where'er I dwell, I dwell with Thee,
In heav'n, in earth, or on the sea;
Where'er I dwell, I dwell with Thee,
In heav'n, in earth, or on the sea;

Prayer

We praise thee, O God, that our religion lies not in what we do or eat or where we go. Thou hast set us free from all externals so that we can elevate ourselves above all these and find Thy heart and worship Thee. Amen.

Seekers After Truth

Jesus saith unto him, I am the way, the truth, and the life:
no man cometh unto the Father, but by me.

JOHN 14:6

In this mixed-up world in which we live there is a group of people claiming to be seekers after truth. "We are seekers after truth," they boast, as if that qualifies them as acceptable worshipers, no matter what their beliefs might be or the truth they are seeking. Some churches actually accommodate this idea and invite people to "come to our church, you do not have to believe anything just be a seeker after truth." This infers a certain openness of mind that accepts anything and everything. In this frame of mind, truth is not absolute but whatever you think of it at the time, or whatever you have determined to be truth.

On the surface, these "seekers after truth" seem to be genuine in their belief or at least heading in the right direction. However, in this day of relativism, truth means different things to different people. What is true to one person may not necessarily be true to another. And what was true yesterday may not be true today. The only thing these "seekers after truth" accomplish is to keep people from seeking the absolute Truth, which is Jesus Christ, "the same yesterday, and today and forever" (Heb. 13:8).

Then there are those who inform us that there is truth in every religion. This is like saying there is water in most poisons, and so it is all right to drink. It is not the water that kills; it is the poison. The more ambiguous the poison, the more dangerous it is. The closer it is to the real thing, the more damage it does. And the enemy of man's soul knows this all too well.

When you study the religions of the world, you will find much in them that is true. However, partial truth is more dangerous than trickery. When I know something is an outright lie, I can stay away from it.

Going back to the Garden of Eden, we see this: The Serpent did not outright lie to Eve; he simply told her partial truth. He only told her what he wanted to tell her in order to mislead her for his advantage. It is what he did not tell her that created all the problems following the Fall in the Garden.

You can tell someone something and not actually lie to him or her, but so present the truth that it keeps this person from the truth.

I can go down to the local zoo and look at a tiger. There it is lying before me, licking itself like a big kitten. Perhaps it is in a playful mood and I can say to myself that this tiger is not dangerous. Why, it is just a big kitty. The tiger can be declawed and all those dangerous teeth extracted. But the partial truth does not change the nature of the tiger. By nature, it is the most efficient killing machine on God's green earth. Its playfulness is only partial truth.

Now, if I approach that tiger accepting only partial truth, I am putting myself in mortal danger. It is what you do not know that can hurt you.

Those who boast that they are seekers after truth are putting themselves and others at greater risk than I would face in the tiger's pen. The tiger can only harm the body; but these partial religious truths can effectively lead me into everlasting spiritual darkness and final damnation.

Every false religion in the world has a base of truth about it. It starts with some truth and then moves away from it subtly and maliciously, though maybe not intentionally. Eve did not intentionally disobey God or knowingly move away from ultimate truth.

When it comes to the worship of God, we must be quite careful that we are not basing it on partial truth, but on the entire revealed truth such as can be found in the Bible.

Man wants to worship God, but he wants to worship God after his own comprehension of truth. So did Cain, so did the Samaritans and so have men and women down the years; but God has rejected it all. Now, there is an imperative to worship deep within the heart of mankind, but with God, there is no tolerance, there is no broad spirit. There is the sharp pinpointing of fact so that every man in his own fallacy is completely rejected.

I have piles of religious poetry, and I have read most of it. People who have not found God, and have not experienced the new birth and the Holy Spirit on them, still have the ancient impulse to worship something. If they come from a third-world country where there is little education, they might kill a chicken, put a feather on their head and dance around a fire, calling for a witch doctor. However, if they have some education, they write poetry.

Edwin Markham (1852-1940) was an American poet who wrote two or three good things. He wrote "Lincoln" and "The Man with the Hoe," and that is good poetry. However, I quote him because this is an example of the way the human mind goes. The world is full of bushel baskets of poetry like this that you can throw out; the kind of poetry and religion that has no anchor, no God, no High Priest, no blood, no altar, but floats around like a drunken butterfly, floating and flopping about not knowing quite where he wants to go, and they all say about the same thing.

> I made a pilgrimage to find the God;
> I listened for His voice at holy tombs,
> Searched for the prints of His immortal feet
> In the dust of broken altars; yet turned back
> With empty heart. But on the homeward road
> A great light came upon me and I heard
> The God's voice ringing in a nesting lark;
> Felt His sweet wonder in a growing rose;
> Received His blessing from a wayside well;
> Looked on His beauty in a lover's face;
> Saw His bright hand send signal from the sun.

He was a good poet in many regards, but his ornithology was not very sound. In the first place, nesting larks do not sing. In the second place, he said that he heard God singing like a bird. Then he said, "I felt his sweet wonder in a swaying rose and received his blessing from a wayside well. Looked on his beauty in a lover's face. Saw His bright hand send signals from the sun."

There you have it: not a crazy man and not a medicine man from the jungles of New Guinea. Here is a man whose poetry is in every anthology. He writes among the poets of the world and goes out looking for God. And he searched for Him in the first place, a graveyard, and did not find Him. He looked at broken altars and could not find Him there; then on the way back, he hears a bird singing and says that it is God. And he sees a happy lover holding hands with his girlfriend and says that's God. And he sees a rose waving in the wind and he says that's God. So he comes home and writes himself a poem.

Now, I want to know, how could he get this bad? How could this man, in a land of Bibles, with the gospel being preached, write that he went looking for God in altars and tombs and in all dark, dusty places, yet didn't find Him? And started home and saw him and heard him singing in a nesting lark; saw him in a rose and saw him in the face of a young lover? Then he looked up and, lo and behold, God was signaling from the sun. I never had any signals from the sun myself, and I do not know of anybody except Edwin Markham who wrote about this.

This kind of thing, it seems to me, needs to be exposed. We need to tell the world that God is Spirit, and they that worship Him must worship Him in spirit and in truth. It must be the Holy Spirit and truth. You cannot worship Him in Spirit alone, for the Spirit without truth is helpless. It cannot be in truth alone, for that would be theology without fire. It must be the truth of God and the Spirit of God.

When a man, yielding and believing the truth of God, is full with the Spirit of God, then his warmest and smallest whisper will be worship. So, we can find that we will worship God by any means if we are full of the Spirit and yielded to the truth. However, when we are yielded to neither the truth nor full of the Spirit, there is no worship at all. God cannot receive into His holy heart just any kind of worship.

Jesus said, "they that worship Him must worship in spirit and in truth" and settled forever how we should worship God. God formed the living flame, and He gave the reasoning mind that only He may claim the worship of mankind. But instead of our worshiping God, every man worships after his own fashion.

Keep in mind, there is only one way to worship God: "I am the way, the truth, and the life: no man cometh unto the Father, but by me" (John 14:6). Instead of being kindly and charitable by allowing an idea to stand that God accepts worship from anybody, anywhere, we are actually injuring and jeopardizing the future of the man or woman we allow to get away with that. Anything incompatible with the holy nature of God only damages a man's soul and ultimately damns that soul forever.

I would do as seventeenth-century hymn writer Isaac Watts did when he tried to put the psalms in meter. He just could not leave a psalm if there was nothing about Jesus in it. He would always put in a stanza about Jesus before he was through. Personally, I am glad he did.

It is an either/or situation. Either a worshiper must submit to God's truth or he cannot worship God at all. A person can write poems and he can get elevations of thought when he sees a sunrise. He can hear the fledgling lark sing, but fledgling larks do not sing. And he can do all sorts of things, but he cannot worship God except in faith. To do so would mean that he has to surrender to the revealed truth about God. He has to confess that God is who He says He is and He is what He says He is. And he has to declare that Christ is who He says He is and what He says He is. He has to own up to the truth about himself and admit that he is as bad a sinner as God says he is. Then he must acknowledge the truth of the atonement, the blood of Jesus Christ that cleanses and delivers from sin. Finally, he has to come God's way. He must be renewed after the image of He that created him.

Only the redeemed man can worship God acceptably. Only the renewed man can worship God acceptably and embrace the truth as God has revealed it in His Word.

So these people who have churches and pray in the name of the "all good" and the "all Father" have no idea of what true worship that is acceptable in the eyes of God is, and they stumble in spiritual darkness. I would rather go out in the park and walk with my New Testament. I can find my God, not the god in a rose but the God who sits on the throne on high and by His side sits the one whose name is Jesus, having all power in heaven and in earth. And I could commune with God walking out on the street rather than worship Him at an altar of Baal.

Man must be renewed. He must have an infusion of the Spirit of truth. Without an infusion of the Holy Ghost, there can be no true worship.

How big God is and how comprehensive is the work of Christ! How imperative is repentance and regeneration in the Holy Spirit! By rejecting the Holy Spirit, we put out our eyes and blunder on in darkness, sightless and lost. Let us not be guilty of that in this day of open Bibles and plenty of truth.

Bernard of Clairvaux (1091–1153), in his great hymn, expresses the heart of all those who are truly seeking after truth.

> Jesus, Thou Joy of loving hearts,
> Thou Fount of life, Thou Light of men,
> From the best bliss that earth imparts,
> We turn unfilled to Thee again.
> Thy truth unchanged hath ever stood;
> Thou savest those that on Thee call;
> To them that seek Thee Thou art good,
> To them that find Thee all in all.
> We taste Thee, O Thou living Bread,
> And long to feast upon Thee still;
> We drink of Thee, the Fountainhead,
> And thirst our souls from Thee to fill.
> Our restless spirits yearn for Thee,
> Where'er our changeful lot is cast;
> Glad when Thy gracious smile we see,
> Blessed when our faith can hold Thee fast.
> O Jesus, ever with us stay,
> Make all our moments calm and bright;
> Chase the dark night of sin away,
> Shed over the world Thy holy light.

Prayer

O God, how wonderful is the work of Thy Son. It fills the whole universe with wonder and awe and admiration. My heart is overwhelmed with the intensity of that work within me. I seek Thee, but I only find Thee when I have sought Thee with my whole heart and mind. My wonderment at Thee has all but exhausted my expressions of praise and worship. Thy presence is my comfort day and night. Amen.

WHAT CAME FIRST: WORKERS OR WORSHIPERS?

I believe in one God, the Father Almighty, Maker of heaven and earth, and of all things visible and invisible. And in one Lord Jesus Christ, the only-begotten Son of God, begotten of the Father before all worlds; God of God, Light of Light, very God of very God; begotten, not made. . . .

NICENE CREED

Thou art the King of Glory, O Christ, thou art the everlasting Son of the Father. When thou tookest upon thee to deliver man, thou didst humble thyself to be born of a Virgin. When thou hadst overcome the sharpness of death, thou didst open the Kingdom of Heaven to all believers.

TE DEUM LAUDAMUS

These ancient assertions or creeds, as they are sometimes called, were made by the church down the centuries, declaring herself with great joy and a sense of deep unworthiness. I join my voice with theirs and say that I believe these things and I believe that He, the King of Glory, everlasting Son of the Father took upon

Him to deliver man and overcame the sharpness of death and the resurrection and is now opened the Kingdom of heaven to all believers.

In light of this, the human mind must give answer to some questions. One of those questions is why did all of this take place? God of gods and Light of light, He was born of a virgin, suffered under Pontius Pilate, overcame the sharpness of death and opened the Kingdom of heaven to all believers. Back of this must be a purpose, for God has intellect. Intellect is one of the attributes of deity and, therefore, God must have a reasonable purpose that can stand up under the scrutiny of sanctified human reason. Why did God do all of this?

As an evangelical, I am deeply worried and concerned to the point of some degree of suffering over the state of evangelicals these days. By evangelicals, I mean the free churches generally—the churches that have order, those that do not have order and the ones that have disorder. The churches that have beautiful services and plain services, hit-and-miss and off-the-cuff services, and churches whose ministers feel they must be a cross between the apostle Paul, Moses and Bob Hope.

The supreme reason the Lord was born of the Virgin Mary to suffer under Pontius Pilate to be crucified, die and be buried; the reason He overcame death and rose again from the grave is that He might make worshipers out of rebels. We are the recipients of a grace meant to save us from self-centeredness and make worshipers out of us.

Thomas Boston said the difference between man and beast is that a beast looks down and a man is made to look up. A man can engage the God above while the beast goes about and only sees the ground underneath its short legs. But man can see into the heavens above. A beast bows under his burden, but a man lifts his heart in praise to his Burden bearer, Jesus Christ.

God is infinitely more concerned that He has worshipers than that He has workers. Unfortunately, most evangelicals do not share this concern. For the most part, evangelicals have been reduced to the position where God is a supervisor desperately seeking help. Standing at the wayside, He tries to find how many helpers will come to His rescue and bail Him out of a tight spot. We mistakenly believe that God needs workers, and so we cheerfully say, "I'll go to work for the Lord." If we could only remember that as far as His plans are concerned, God does not need us.

I think we should work for the Lord, but it is a matter of grace on God's part. However, I do not think we should ever work until we learn to worship. A worshiper can work with eternal quality in his work but a worker who does not worship is only piling up wood, hay and stubble for the time when God sets the world on fire. God wants worshipers before He wants workers. He calls us back to that for which we were created—to worship the Lord God and to enjoy Him forever. And then out of our deep worship flows our work for Him. Our work is only acceptable to God if our worship is acceptable.

Many of the great hymns of the church came out of revival of some kind. They can be traced through the Lutheran Reformation, the Wesleyan Revival and the Moravian Revival. These hymns were born out of the times when the church of God labored. The Spirit fell upon it, heaven was opened and she saw visions of God; radiance beamed from the throne above reflected from the hearts of His people.

If the devil has a sense of humor, I think he must laugh and hold his sooty sides when he sees a church of dead Christians singing a hymn written by a spiritually awakened and worshiping composer. Many great hymns I didn't like in my early days, because I heard them sung in some dead prayer meeting with a dead song leader who did not expect anything, and a dead congregation in front of him who did not expect anything. Both would have been shocked if anything happened. They had a spirit of no expectation. True worship that is pleasing to God creates within the human heart a spirit of expectation and insatiable longing.

We must understand that the Holy Spirit only descends on a heart engaged in worship. Out of your fiery worship, God will call you to work for Him. But He is not interested in you jumping up and starting some slapdash religious project. This is where the contemporary church is today. Any untrained, unprepared, spiritually empty rattletrap of a fellow who is a bit ambitious can start something religious, like The Fig-Leaf Gospel Tabernacle. People listen to him and work to try to help this man who never heard from God in the first place. Many confuse this wild amateurism as spiritually dynamic worship and offer it to God. From my point of view, nobody who worships God is likely to do anything offbeat or out of place. Nobody who is a true worshiper is likely to give himself up to carnal and worldly religious projects.

Every glimpse we have of worshiping creatures or of heaven show people worshiping. I read Ezekiel 1:1-28, and think about these strange, beautiful creatures with wings, high and lifted up; creatures that put down their wings and drop quietly by the throne of God in reverent worship. At the voice of the Lord, they raised their wings, and their faces stayed straight forward and did not turn where they went (see v. 12). I love that too. This is a glorious picture of the creatures and God's people worshiping in ecstatic wonder and adoration.

Then you find in Isaiah, the sixth chapter, an account of rapturous worship. "In the year that King Uzziah died, I saw the Lord sitting upon a throne, high and lifted up, and His train filled the temple. Above it stood the seraphims: each one had six wings; with twain he covered his face; and with twain he covered his feet . . ." (Isa. 6:1-2). They answered each other antiphonally, and they said, "Holy, holy, holy is the LORD of Hosts: the whole earth is full of his glory" and the temple was filled with the incense, and the temple doors shook, or pillars shook (vv. 3-4). They were worshiping God in joyous and awesome wonder. Not irreverent, emotional outbursts that serve only to stroke the flesh.

Worship is also found in the book of Revelation (4:9-11): "And when those beasts give glory and honour and thanks to him that sat on the throne, who liveth for ever and ever, the four and twenty elders fall down before him that sat on the throne and worship him that liveth for ever and ever, and cast their crowns before the throne, saying, 'Thou art worthy, O Lord, to receive glory and honour and power: for thou hast created all things, and for thy pleasure they are and were created.'"

A little further on, "Every creature which is in heaven, and on earth, and under the earth, and such as are in the sea, and all that are in them, heard I them saying, Blessing, and honor, and glory, and power, be unto him that sitteth upon the throne, and unto the Lamb forever and ever. And the four beasts said, Amen. And the four and twenty elders fell down and worshipped him that liveth forever and ever" (Rev. 5:13-14).

I see a wonderful picture of some class of being called elders. I do not know whether they are elders such as we elect in our churches or not. Then there are beasts, which otherwise are called living creatures. They are all worshiping the Lord God, and wherever you look in heaven, you will find them engaged in worship. If worship bores you, you are not ready for heaven. Worship is the very atmosphere of heaven focusing on the person of Jesus Christ.

I believe in justification by faith as strongly as Martin Luther ever did. I believe that we are only saved by faith in the Son of God as Lord and Savior. But what concerns me is an automatic quality about being saved nowadays. It works something like this: simply put a nickel of faith in the slot, pull down a lever and take out the little coin of salvation, tuck it in your pocket and off you go. It is that simple. After that, you say you are saved. When questioned, you simply say, "I put the nickel in; I accepted Jesus and I signed the card." Very good, there is nothing wrong with signing a card so that we can know who they are. It is the only way we know that some people are Christians. How tragic.

Christianity is not a result of coming to God and becoming an automatic cookie-cutter Christian, stamped out with a die: "One size fits all"; "What God has done for others He'll do for you." These are marvelous mottos with a grain of truth in them, but they lead us far from the absolute truth. We come to Christ so that we might be individually redeemed and made in the image of Christ—vibrant, personal Christians who love God with all our heart and worship Him in the beauty of holiness.

Not only is worship the normal employment for moral beings, but worship is also the moral imperative. The book of Luke tells us that when they came nigh the mount of Olives, the whole multitude of the disciples began to rejoice and praise God with a loud voice for all the mighty works that they had seen (see Luke 19:37).

Some people believe they are worshiping when they are making a lot of noise and chatter and racket. They can never worship without noise and commotion. Religious noise and worship do not necessarily mean the same thing.

On the other side, I want to warn you cultured, quiet, self-possessed, poised, sophisticated people so sure of yourself that it embarrasses you if anybody says "Amen" out loud in a church meeting. Throughout history, the people of God have always been a little bit noisy.

I often think of that dear English saint going back 600 years—Lady Julian of Norwich. She was meditating on how high and lofty Jesus was and yet how He "meeked" Himself down to the lowest part of our human desire, and she just could not control herself. She let go with a shout and prayed aloud in Latin, which translated into English meant, "Well, glory to God! Isn't this a marvelous thing?!"

If that bothers you, something is wrong.

Our Lord was faced with such criticism: "And when he was come nigh, even now at the descent of the mount of Olives, the whole multitude of the disciples began to rejoice and praise God with a loud voice for all the mighty works that they had seen" (Luke 19:37). I am quite sure they were not in tune. When you get a crowd of people whom the Lord has blessed, and when they go out of themselves with worship and joy, they are just as likely as not to praise God a little bit off key.

"Saying, Blessed be the King that cometh in the name of the Lord: peace in heaven, and glory in the highest. And some of the Pharisees from among the multitude said unto him, Master, rebuke thy disciples" (vv. 38-39). It offended the Pharisees to hear anybody sing glory to God aloud. So they said to Jesus, "Master, rebuke thy disciples."

"And he answered and said unto them, I tell you that, if these should hold their peace, the stones would immediately cry out" (v. 40). Jesus said, in effect, that He was to be worshiped. Those Pharisees would have died in their tracks if they had heard a rock praising the Lord. These poor people were praising God at the top of their voices.

Worship is a moral imperative, and yet I believe that it is the missing jewel in evangelical circles. The crown is here but the jewels are missing. The church has decked herself with every ornament, but one shining gem is missing—the jewel of worship.

This has practical implications in the local church. For example, a man who will never attend a prayer meeting finds himself on the church board, making decisions for the entire church. He would never go to a prayer meeting because he is not a worshiper; he is just a fellow who runs the church; and in his mind, he can separate the two. My brother, you cannot separate the two.

I do not believe that any man has a right to debate a church issue or vote on it unless he is a praying, worshiping man. Only a worshiping man has the ability to make spiritual decisions within the context of the local church. If we are not worshipers, we are wasting other people's money and only piling up wood, hay and stubble to be burned at the last day. It might be business as usual, but it is not glorious worship.

Worship is an awesome thing, and I would rather worship God than any other thing I know of in the entire world.

If you were to go to my study, you would discover piles of hymnbooks. As a singer, I leave a lot to be desired; but that is nobody's business. My singing is an expression of my worship of the Almighty God above. God listens while I sing to Him old French hymns and translations of the old Latin hymns and old Greek hymns from the Eastern Church; and of course, the beautiful songs done in meter as well as some of the simpler songs of Watts and Wesley and the rest. The Christian hymnal is a beautiful place to begin a daily regimen of worshiping God.

Some might point out that it is a waste of time to spend your time worshiping God. "There is work to be done for the Master," we are told. There is no time for loafing, as though worship was in the category of loafing. The beautiful part about this is, if you worship God, you will be an active person.

People ablaze with the radiant worship of God did every deed done in the church of Christ. The great mystics, the great hymn writers and the great saints were the ones doing all the work. The saints who wrote the great hymns that we sing were active to the point where you wondered how they ever did it. George Whitefield, John and Charles Wesley, Bernard of Clairvaux, Gerhard Tersteegen and others wrote our hymns of faith. The more intense their worship the more extended their work. Hospitals grew out of the hearts of worshiping men. Insane asylums grew out of the heart of worshiping men. Worshiping men and women learned to be compassionate to those whose minds had failed them.

Look at some of the great advances in civilizations and you will discover they were made by worshiping men and women. Whenever the church came out of her lethargy and rose from her spiritual slumber and into a renaissance and revival, worshipers were always back of it all.

We are called to worship, and we are failing God when we are not worshiping to the fullness of our redeemed potential. When we substitute worship with work, we are failing God in ways that we can hardly imagine. When the glory of God came down on the Temple in olden days, the priest could not stand and minister, such was the awesome presence of God.

When a traveling salesman got to the town where Charles Finney's revival was going on in New England, he sensed that something was happening. The first man he met he inquired about it. He was told, "There's a revival in this town; God is here and people are being converted, saloons are being closed up, halfway houses are being nailed shut. Men and women are cleaning up. Evil men are quitting their daily habits and getting right with God. God's in this place."

This is what we lack in evangelical churches. We do not have it in our Bible conferences, in our camp meetings or in our churches. Most churches today are run the way you would run a club or business, and it grieves my heart. I wish we might get back again to worship so that when people entered church, they would find God's people worshiping and fall on their faces and say, "Truly God is in this place."

The presence of the Lord is the most wonderful thing in the entire world. I once prayed under a tree with some preachers and a Salvation Army captain. I prayed and the others prayed. Then the Salvation Army man began to pray. I cannot remember a word he said, but I knew that here was a man engaging God in an awesome, marvelous, elevated feeling in the holy act of worship.

As a lad, I belonged to a very liberal church. At the time, I did not know any better. One Sunday night, a little girl got up to sing. She was a hunchback and had a face that looked as if she had suffered a lot. Her appearance did not generate much expectation, at least from me. However, when she began to sing, something changed. What a beautiful little face she had. She stood there and sang with a child's voice. She was worshiping God.

This is missing in the churches. We used to sing an old hymn written by Isaac Watts.

Bless, O my soul, the living God,
Call home thy thoughts that rove abroad:
Let all the powers within me join
In work and worship so divine,
In work and worship so divine.

Bless, O my soul, the God of grace;
His favors claim thy highest praise;
Why should the wonders He hath wrought
Be lost in silence and forgot,
Be lost in silence and forgot?

"Why should the wonders He hath wrought be lost in silence and forgot?" Why should we be silent about the wonders of God? "Why should the wonders that He hath wrought be lost in silence and forgot?" Let the whole earth His power confess; let the whole earth adore His grace. The Gentiles with the Jews shall join in worship and work so divine.

That is what a church is supposed to be, not a big ecclesiastical machine with someone turning the crank with a big smile you could not wipe off, who loves everybody and everybody loves him. He has the building to pay for, and he turns the crank and the machine runs. Oh, this kind of thing grieves my heart. I want to be among worshipers. I want to be among a people who know the presence of God in their midst, resulting in radiant and sometimes ecstatic worship.

Prayer

Dear Lord Jesus, we love Thee and we love Thy Holy Father. We love the blessed Holy Ghost, the Comforter, the Lord and giver of life who with the Father and Son together is worshiped and glorified; we love Thee, O God. We expect to spend eternity with Thee, not standing in behind, worshiping the altar, but like the creatures out of the fire worshiping with trembling joy and then rising to go and do Thy service somewhere in the far reaches of the Creation and hurrying back to the Throne to report, O God.

We look forward to this; we used to feel that death is a terrible, dark, ugly, cruel river; but in another way it's a

*door into a new light, and we love to look upon Thy face and
see Thy people, see Abraham and Isaac and Jacob, and sit
down in the kingdom of God with thy people and every
tongue and tribe and nation around the world. O Lord,
prepare us now for that hour. Teach us the protocol of heaven;
teach us the etiquette of the kingdom. Teach us now so
that we will not be doing anything strange when we pick up
our harp and join the company innumerable or sing in the
choir invisible. Bless this people, Lord. Holy Ghost with light
divine, shine upon this heart of mine. Holy Ghost with power
divine, come we pray Thee, and give power and grace and
strength to these hearts of ours, for Christ's sake.*

The Components of True Worship

And the glory which thou gavest me I have given them;
that they may be one, even as we are one.

John 17:22

Worship is not confined to emotion and feelings but is an inward attitude and a state of mind subject to degrees of perfection and intensity. It is not possible to always worship with the same degree of wonder and love as at other times, but wonder and love always has to be there.

A father may not always love his family with the same intensity when he is tired and his business is having trouble. Although he may not have a feeling of love toward his family, still it is there because it is not a feeling only; it is an attitude and a state of mind and a sustained act subject to varying degrees of intensity and perfection.

With this in mind, I want to give you a definition of worship as it ought to be found in the church. It embodies a number of factors or ingredients, both spiritual and emotional.

A Definition of Worship

First, worship is to feel in the heart. I use that word "feel" boldly and without apology. I do not believe that we are to be a feeling-less people. I came into the kingdom of God the old-fashioned way. I believe that I know something of the emotional life that goes with being converted; so I believe in feeling. I do not think we should follow feeling, but I believe that if there is no feeling in our heart, then we are dead. If you woke up in the morning and suddenly had no feeling in your right arm, you would call a doctor. You would dial with the left hand because your right hand was dead. Anything that has no feeling in it, you can be quite sure is dead. Real worship, among other things, is a feeling in the heart.

Worship is to feel in the heart and express in some appropriate manner a humbling but delightful sense of admiring awe. Worship will humble a person as nothing else can. The egotistical, self-important man cannot worship God any more than the arrogant devil can worship God. There must be humility in the heart before there can be worship.

When the Holy Spirit comes and opens heaven until people stand astonished at what they see, and in astonished wonderment confess His uncreated loveliness in the presence of that most ancient mystery, then you have worship. If it is not mysterious, there can be no worship; if I can understand God, then I cannot worship God.

I will never get on my knees and say, "Holy, holy, holy" to that which I can figure out. That which I can explain will never overawe me, never fill me with astonishment, wonder or admiration. But in the presence of that most ancient mystery, that unspeakable majesty, which the philosophers have called a *mysterium tremendum*, which we who are God's children call "our Father which art in heaven," I will bow in humble worship. This attitude ought to be present in every church today.

Blaise Pascal (1623–1662) was one of the greatest minds that ever lived. When he was only in his teens, he wrote advanced books on mathematics, astonishing people. He became a great philosopher, mathematician and thinker.

One night, he met God, and his whole world was changed. He wrote down his experience on a piece of paper while it was still fresh in his mind. According to his testimony, from 10:30 P.M. to about 12:30 A.M., he was overwhelmed by the presence of God. To express what he was experiencing, he wrote one word, "fire."

Pascal was neither a fanatic nor an ignorant farmer with hayseeds back of his ears. He was a great intellectual. God broke through all that and for two solid hours, he experienced something he could only characterize later as fire.

Following his experience, he prayed; and to keep as a reminder of that experience, he wrote it out: "God of Abraham, God of Isaac, God of Jacob, not of the philosophers and of the learned." This was not a prayer for somebody who reads his prayers; this was not formal religious ritual. This was the ecstatic utterance of a man who had two wonderful, awesome hours in the presence of his God. "God of Abraham, God of Isaac, God of Jacob not of the philosophers and of the learned. God of Jesus Christ. . . . Thy God shall be my God. Forgetfulness of the world and of everything, except God. . . . He is only found by the ways taught in the Gospel. . . . Righteous Father, the world has not known Thee, but I have known Thee. Joy, joy, joy, tears of joy. . . ." And he put an "Amen" after that, folded it up, put it in his shirt pocket and kept it there.

That man could explain many mysteries in the world, but he was awestruck before the wonder of wonders, even Jesus Christ. His worship flowed out of his encounter with that "fire" and not out of his understanding of who and what God is.

Four Ingredients of Worship

I have given a running definition of worship; now I want to define four major factors or ingredients in worship.

Confidence

Many cannot rightly worship these days because they do not have a high enough opinion of God. In our mind, God has been reduced, modified, edited, changed, amended until He does not resemble the God Isaiah saw high and lifted up, but something else again. And because He has been reduced in the minds of the people, they do not have that boundless confidence in his character that marked a former generation of Christians.

Confidence is necessary to respect. Without confidence in a man, it is difficult to respect him. Extend that upward to God. If we cannot respect Him, it becomes impossible to worship Him. In the church today, our worship rises and falls altogether depending upon whether the idea of God is low or high. We must always begin with God where everything begins. Everywhere and always God has to be antecedent; God is always there first, always previous, always prior. The God who is there is not the homemade cheap god you can buy these days marked down because He's shelf-worn. However, the God and Father, the awesome God, the mysterious God, the God who watches over the world and holds the universe in His great hands, this God we must worship.

One thing needed in this time is a reformation of worship. Our concepts of God must be rescued from the deplorable depths they have sunk. God needs no rescue, but we must rescue our concepts from their fallen and frightfully inadequate condition that hinders pure and delightful worship.

Boundless confidence is one thing. Without absolute confidence in God, I cannot worship Him. It is impossible to sit down with a man and have fellowship with him if you have reason to fear that he is out to get you or is tricking or deceiving or cheating you. You have to respect Him before you can sit down quietly and enjoy mutual fellowship, which is the core of pure worship.

When we go to God, we must raise our affections and our confidence to God. And in the presence of God, we must be without doubt or nervousness or worry or fear that God will cheat us or deceive us or let us down or break His covenant or lie or do something wrong. We have to be convinced to the point where we can go into the presence of God in absolute confidence and say, "Let God be true though every man be a liar." The God of the whole earth cannot do wrong; and when we can do this in the presence of God, it is the beginning of worship.

Admiration

The second component in our worship is admiration.

It is possible to respect a man and not especially admire him. The same would apply to God. Someone may have a theological respect for God that is purely academic while, at the same time, not admire God, or even be unable to admire. But when God made man in His own image, He gave him a capability of appreciation, the ability to appreciate and admire his Creator.

One of the greatest Bible teachers of his generation, Dr. D. Watson, talked often about the love we have for God. He taught two kinds of love: the love of gratitude and the love of excellence. We could love God because we are grateful to Him or we could go on past that and love God because of what He is. It is possible for a child to love his father or mother out of gratitude, which is proper and right; he should, of course. Years later, when he gets to know his parents, or maybe after they are gone, he will remember that he loved them also out of the love of excellence.

Some people we are supposed to love but there is no excellence there. You have to love them with infused love; you cannot love them with a love called out by their excellence. God Almighty is excellent, beyond all other beings. He is excellent; and so this love of excellence surpasses the love of gratitude. God's children rarely get beyond the love they have for Him because He has been good to them. You rarely hear anybody praying in admiration of God and worshiping the excellence of God and talking to God about His own excellence. The psalms do this; Christ did this; and the apostles did, but we do not hear it much now. This generation has produced Christians that are primarily Santa Claus Christians. They eagerly look for God to put up a Christmas tree with all their gifts under it. They are grateful to God, and it is right and proper to be thankful for all things that He does for us and all the good, large and small, that He gives us. That is, however, only the lower, elementary kind of love.

Going beyond that comes the love of excellence where you can go into the presence of God and not want to rush out again, but stay in the presence of God, because you are in the presence of utter, infinite excellence. Naturally, you admire this, and this knowledge can grow until your heart has been lifted into the excellency of love and admiration.

Fascination

The third component I find in worship is fascination.

Fascination is to be full of moral excitement. You cannot read your Bible very long until you find that God fascinated some people. They were fascinated by Him and were filled with a high moral excitement. It would be difficult to find much of this today in the average church in America.

Wherever God is known indeed by the Holy Spirit illumination, there is a fascination and a high moral excitement. There is a fascination captured, charmed, and entranced by the presence and person of God. To be fascinated is to be struck with astonished wonder at the inconceivable elevation and magnitude and splendor of God.

For me it is either God or agnosticism. I do not know many churches I would want to join and get into the rat race. I do not want to be part of any religious group where each person is merely a cog in the wheel: the pastor turns the crank, and if it comes out all right in the end of the year and there is no deficit, he is a good man. I am not interested in that at all. I want to begin with God and end with God. Of course, I can never end with God, because there is no end in Him.

Many of the hymns of the church came out of this sense of admiration and fascination in the hearts of men.

"Oh, Jesus, Jesus, dearest Lord, forgive me if I say for very love Thy precious name a thousand times a day." That came out of a man, Fredrick W. Faber (1814–1863), fascinated by what he saw. He admired God until he was charmed and struck with wonder at the inconceivable elevation and magnitude and moral splendor of this being we call God.

Adoration

The fourth component of worship is adoration.

Adoration is white heat made incandescent with the fire of the Holy Spirit, and it is to love with all the powers within us. It is to feel, to love with fear, wonder, yearning and awe. I shudder when I think of how many are doing things today in regards to worship in the church completely counter to this spirit of adoration. Adoration cannot be conjured up by the manipulation of some worship leader.

Sure, they preach about Jesus dying for us, and say, "Now, if you believe that and accept Him, everything will be all right." But there is no fascination, no admiration, no adoration, no love, no fear, no wonder, no yearning, no awe, no longing, no hunger and no thirst. I wonder if they really have met God at all. How could they and not be elevated into the holy atmosphere of adoration?

A young couple has their first baby, and lays its little warm, pitching, kicking form in the cradle. They love their baby and continue to love it. They love it because it is alive. There never was a doll made anywhere by the most skillful artist, the most beautifully and human looking thing that could bring out the shining-eyed wonder in a couple's face that a newborn baby can bring out. It does not have to be pretty; it just has to be their baby, alive, warm and breathing. There is no difference between this mechanical "nickel-in-the-slot" Christianity passing for Christianity now and that Christianity of our fathers, where men worshiped God in awful wonder and adoration.

Bishop James Usher would go down by the bank of the river on a Saturday and spend the afternoon on his knees in the presence of God, in awesome worship. Jonathan Edwards' son-in-law, David Brainerd, would kneel in the snow and be so lost in worship, prayer and intercession that when he was through the snow would be melted around him in a wide circle. John Fletcher, the saint of Methodism, used to kneel in his little bare room on the floor. When he lived out his life and had gone to be with God, they found that he had made a concave place in the floor where his knees actually wore out the boards. The walls in his room were stained with his breath where he had waited on God and where he had worshiped his God in the beauty of holiness.

I am very careful when I use the word "adore." I refuse to say about any person, "Oh, I adore him," or "I adore her." I love babies, I love people; but I never adore them. Personally, I use the word "adoration" for the only One who deserves it. In no other presence and before no other being can I kneel in fear, wonder and yearning and feel the sense of possessiveness that cries "mine, mine." There are those who are so theologically stilted that they feel it is not right to say "mine."

I have gone through hymnbooks and in some I have seen where the editors had edited the hymns of Wesley and Watts. They replaced the "I's" and the "me's" and the "mine's" and put "ours." "I love thee, Oh God," is changed to, "We love thee, Oh God."

Because they are so modest, they cannot imagine saying "I," but you will find in worship they cry out, "Oh, God, thou art my God, early will I seek thee," and so it becomes a love experience between God and the person so that it's "I" and "Thee."

Paul was like that and David and Isaiah and Moses and the rest. I desire to possess God; "God is my God"; "the Lord is my shepherd, I shall not want; He maketh me to lie down in green pastures."

Can you imagine what an editor would have done with that: "the Lord is our shepherd, we shall not want, He maketh us to lie down in green pastures." That is togetherness, all right. Therefore, we will all lie down together, but nobody has anything that means "I." You can say "God and I," but you cannot say "us" and mean anything.

Unless you have been able to meet God in loneliness of soul, you and God, as if there is nobody else in the world, you will never know what it is to love other people in the world.

This adoration is the desire to be poured out at God's feet; we desire it; we want to be poured out at God's feet. When trying to elude King Saul, David got a touch of homesickness and said, "Oh that I might have a drink out of the good ole well of Bethlehem, as in my day of my boyhood." One of his men, looking for a promotion, started for the well, risking his life, got some water and brought it back to David. David picked up the cup and said,

"I can't drink this; this is blood. This cost you the rest of your life." So he poured it out as a drink offering unto God.

David knew God enough, had a boundless confidence in God's character and came to admire Him and love Him for His excellence. Consecration is not hard for the person that has met God. This person insists on giving himself entirely to God.

The list I have described—confidence, admiration, fascination, adoration—have these factors in varying degrees of intensity, of course. They condition our thoughts, our words and our deeds. They hallow every place, time and setting, and give back the glory that Christ had before the world. To the Christian, "we in Him and He in us and the glory He had, I have given unto them" (see John 17:22ff).

I read of a creature that God created, who sealed up the sun, and which was filled with wisdom and physical beauty (see Ezek. 28:14-16).

The Old Testament tells us that somewhere out there beyond where the farthest rocket can go, God had a cherub created for that purpose. He was a creature created without embarrassment or fear, burning in the presence of God, covering the stones of fire before the throne. He fell in love with his own beauty, and God said, "Thou art profane." Most Bible teachers believe that this is the devil. The creature was created to worship God, but he turned his worship on himself, and God cast him down.

My concern is that unless we have a real spiritual awakening, and Jesus tarries a while longer, we need missionaries from Africa or China to reintroduce North America to Christianity. God has no particular fondness for nations or buildings or denominations. He longs to be worshiped. When the Church loses her love, she becomes sick.

We are born to worship, and if we are not worshiping God in the beauty of His holiness, we have missed the reason for being born. Worship is a delightful, awesome, humbling, wonderful experience, which we can have in varying degrees, but if you have all those, you can live in the middle of it. You never need to leave church if you are worshipers. You can lock the building and be driven away from the place, but you have not left church at all, because we carry our sanctuary with us; we never leave it.

If you know that your heart is cold, then it is not yet a hard heart; God has not rejected it. Therefore, if there is a yearning within, God put that yearning there. He did not put it there to mock you; He put it there that you might rise to it. God puts the bait of yearning in your heart. He does not turn His back on you; He puts it there because He is there to meet you. Decide now that you are going to get ahead of a spiritually cold way of living.

A wonderful hymn, translated by John Wesley, expresses this thought better than anything I can think of.

Jesus, Thy Boundless Love to Me
by Paul Gerhardt (1607–1676)
Translated by John Wesley

Jesus, Thy boundless love to me
No thought can reach, no tongue declare;
O knit my thankful heart to Thee
And reign without a rival there.
Thine wholly, thine alone I am:
Be thou alone my constant Flame.

Prayer

Our Father, we praise Thee that Thy love indeed is boundless.
Our wretchedness thankfully has great bounds established by
Thy grace and is overcome by the boundlessness of Thy love.
Grant to my heart a true sense of Thy presence.
I pray in Jesus' name. Amen.

THE MYSTERY OF TRUE WORSHIP

And in thy majesty ride prosperously because of truth and meekness and righteousness; and thy right hand shall teach thee terrible things.

PSALM 45:4

In examining the subject of worship, I cannot emphasize enough that mystery surrounds it, and happy the Christian who penetrates and breaks through this mystery. True Christian worship does not rise or fall on the will of man, for there is only one object of worship worthy of man, and that is God.

I wish I could adequately set forth the glory of the object we are to worship. If we could set forth these thousand attributes dwelling in unapproachable light where no man can see Him and live—fully eternal, omniscient, omnipotent and sovereign—we would be greatly humbled. God's people are not as humble as they ought to be, and I believe this is why we do not truly see God in His sovereignty.

We are instructed to worship God, and I wonder how it could be that we Christians would fall on our knees before a man and say, "Thy throne, O God, is forever and ever." That man does not exist before whom I will kneel and say, "God," with one lone supreme exception of the man Christ Jesus—the man whom the prophets saw in the vision and addressed him and said, "Thy throne, O God."

All mystery has about it an ambience of confusion. How can we get out of this state of confusion if there is one God and none other? And how can we say that Jesus Christ is a man and we are taught never to worship man? How can we get down on our knees before Him and worship? Here is the great mystery. I stand bareheaded before it, kneel, take my shoes off my feet before this burning bush and confess I do not understand it. This mystery envelopes my heart, and I bow down in reverence and submission.

Simply put, the mystery is that God and man are united in one person, not two persons. All that is God and all that is man are fused eternally, inexplicably and inseparably in the man, Jesus Christ. When we kneel before the man, Christ Jesus, we are in fact kneeling before God.

The Old Testament illustrates this with Moses before the burning bush. The fire burned in the bush, and the bush was not consumed. Moses instinctively knelt before the bush and worshiped God. Moses understood that God was in the bush. The bush was ordinary until God's presence permeated it and set it aflame. Some could have charged Moses with idolatry— those that could not see the fire in the bush. They could not know the fire he was worshiping was none other than Jehovah.

Suppose there had been some Israelites who knew the teaching from Abraham that one God alone is to be worshiped. Suppose they had seen this man kneeling before a bush with his face in his hands, hiding his face, but they had not been able to see the fire. They would say, and rightly so, "What do you mean worshiping a bush? You are an idolater. Don't you know the Scripture?"

Of course, Moses would have known better. He knew the Scripture, but he knew what the others did not know. He knew that the bush and the fire were united and infused there before him. They were essentially one. There was the nature of the bush and then there was the nature of Jehovah fused into one object. The bush was not consumed and Moses worshiped not the bush but the God who dwells in the bush. Therefore, he knelt before that bush.

I admit that this is an imperfect and inadequate illustration; for as soon as the fire departed from the bush, it was but a bush again and no man could kneel and worship that bush ever again.

This was a picture of the coming of Christ. Christ Jesus was indeed God with all of the full implications of deity. Although Jesus was man in the perfect sense of the word, he was also God in the perfect sense of the word. Jesus Christ in the New Testament is the equivalent of the Old Testament burning bush. The striking difference is, the burning bush was a temporary experience, but Jesus Christ is both God and man for all eternity.

There was never any departure except for that awful moment on the cross when He said, "My God, My God why hast thou forsaken me?" He took all of the putrefying terrible mass of our sin on His holy self and died there. God turned His back on Him but the deity and the humanity never parted, and they remain today united in that one man. When we kneel before

THE PURPOSE OF MAN

that man and say, "My Lord and My God, thy throne O God is for ever and ever," we are talking to God, for by the mystery of the theanthropic union man has become God and God has become man in the person of the Son, Jesus Christ.

We worship this One in mystery and wonder. We worship not man but God in the flesh.

Fusing Meekness and Majesty

If I did not believe the Bible for any other reason, I would believe it for Psalm 45 and Isaiah 53. I would see how the prophets foresaw down the centuries and proclaimed the great mystery of the one called Christ. These men of God described Him as radiantly beautiful and romantic, and as a winsome deity. They said of Him that He was fair, He was royal, He was gracious, He was majestic, He was true, He was meek, righteous, loving, glad and fragrant. Human language was exhausted in trying to set forth the opulence of this One we call Christ; and after a while, even the prophets gave up trying to describe Him.

If I were searching the dictionary to find words to describe something or somebody, I would be glad to kneel before this: He is fair and He is kingly, and yet He is gracious. He is not a king who stands in His dignity and looks down his nose at the world, but He is a gracious king. His graciousness does not take away from His majesty; He is true and He is meek. *Meekness and majesty*. I would like to write a hymn or a book about it or maybe paint a picture or compose music about it—the meekness and majesty of Jesus. You do not find meekness and majesty united very much. The meekness was His humanity, and the majesty was His deity. He was a human being like any other human being, but He was God, and in His majesty He stood before Herod and before Pilate. And when He comes down from the sky, it will be in His majesty, the majesty of God; and yet it will be the majesty of the man who is God.

Our Lord Jesus Christ is majestic and meek. Before His foes, He stands in majesty; and before His friends, He bows in meekness. You can experience either side you want. If you choose not the meek side of Jesus, you will experience the majestic side of Jesus. The harlots came to Him, and the babies, and the publicans, and the sick, and the bleeding woman, and the devil-possessed man. They came from everywhere, touched Him and found Him so meek that His power went out to them and healed them.

I do not think you have to be very fanciful or poetic when you talk about worshiping the Lord in the beauty of holiness if you know that you are talking about something that will please the heavenly host.

Fused in the person of Christ is all the beauty and wonderment of God, enabling us to worship God in the beauty of holiness. The tremendous aspect of this worship is that we can worship God wherever Jesus is. Wherever we find Him is the perfect place to worship. I cannot explain this mystery; I only can revel in it and kneel before this eternal burning bush.

Portable Worship

Why is it that when we think of worship, we think of something we do when we go to church? God's poor stumbling, bumbling people; how confused we can get, and stay confused for a lifetime and die confused. Books are written confusing us further, and we write songs to confirm the books and confuse ourselves and others even further; and we do it all as if the only place one can worship God is in a church building we call the house of God. We enter the house dedicated to God, made out of bricks, linoleum and other stuff, and we say, "The Lord is in His holy temple; let all kneel before Him."

I personally enjoy starting a service that way occasionally. But it does not stop there. Come 9:00 A.M. Monday morning, if you do not walk into your office and say, "The Lord is in my office and all the world is silent before Him," then you were not worshiping the Lord on Sunday. If you cannot worship Him on Monday, then you did not worship Him on Sunday. If you do not worship Him on Saturday, your worship on Sunday is not authentic. Some people put God in a box we call the church building. God is not present in church any more than He is present in your home. God is not here any more than He is in your factory or office.

As a young Christian, I worked for the BF Goodrich Company in Akron, Ohio, helping to make rubber tires. I worshiped God at my assembly line station until I had tears in my eyes. Nobody ever saw the tears or asked me about them, but I would not have hesitated to tell them why.

As I went along and worked a while at something, it became automatically converted to thinking about something else. Some daydream; I worshiped. I got to where I could do my work with passing skill and worship God at the same time. God was at my work just as much as He was at my church. As far as I was concerned, there was no difference. If God is not in your factory, if God is not in your store, if God is not in your office, then God is not in your church when you go there. When we worship our God, the breath of songs on Earth starts the organs playing in heaven above.

The total life, the whole man and woman, must worship God. Faith, love, obedience, loyalty, conduct and life—all of these are to worship God. If there is anything in you that does not worship God, then there is not anything in you that does worship God very well. If you departmentalize your life and let certain parts worship God, but other parts do not worship God, then you are not worshiping God as you should. It is a great delusion we fall into, the idea that in church or in the presence of death or in the midst of sublimity is the only setting for worship.

You carry worship inside your heart. You can have your worship with you. I have been with people who became very spiritual when standing on a mountain looking down. I remember being caught in a storm one time in the mountains in Pennsylvania, and I could see it out there. I don't remember how many miles away they told us it was—I think it was 50 miles from where we were—but you could see it out there. We huddled up against a rock while the storm and the hailstones hit us. They came rattling and roaring down on us, and we huddled against the car against the rock of that great storm in its white fury over the mountain.

I do not have to see a storm on a mountain to make me know how jealous God is. The stars and their courses tell about it, and the babe that cries yonder tells about it; the flower that blooms by the way tells about it and the fine snow that drifts down tells about it. We do not have to have it dramatically brought home to us for it to be true. It is a great delusion to think that because we feel a sense of the poetic in the presence of a storm or the stars or a mountain that we are spiritual. That is not necessarily true at all, because murderers, tyrants and drunkards also can feel like that.

There never was a drunkard that when he came to himself did not have such feelings, and there never was a tyrant after giving the command to slay a dozen men, on his way home might see something that would raise poetic worship in him. That is not imagined; that is worship, my brethren.

Worship pleasing to God saturates our whole being. There is no worship pleasing to God until there is nothing in me displeasing to God. I cannot departmentalize my life, worship God on Sunday and not worship Him on Monday. I cannot worship Him in my songs and displease Him in my business engagements. I cannot worship God in silence in the church on Sunday, to the sound of hymns, then go out on the next day and be displeasing to Him in my activities. No worship is wholly pleasing to God until there is nothing in us that is displeasing to God.

Without Jesus Christ, there is no goodness, and so I do not apologize at all when I say that your worship has to be all-inclusive and take you all in. If you are not worshiping God in all your life, then you are not worshiping Him acceptably in any area of your life.

Worship Disciplines

Although worship is a natural desire of Christians, there are disciplines we must employ. I believe that personal preparation is essential in our worship of God. That preparation is not always a pleasant thing and must include some revolutionary changes. Some things must be destroyed in your life. The gospel of Jesus Christ is not only constructive, but it is also destructive, destroying certain elements in you that should not be there, impeding worship. The fire in the burning bush only consumed those elements that should not be there. And so, as we yield ourselves to the operations of the Holy Spirit, He will begin routing out those elements in our life that impede worship; and that is both satisfying to us and acceptable to God.

Pray in the Nature of Jesus

For example, many are hampered in their worship by the inclusion of magic. Certain words and phrases carry some magical essence for some people. There is no magic in faith and no magic in the name of Jesus. Reciting certain phrases or even certain special verses of Scripture has no miraculous effect in our life. This is what the Bible refers to as vain repetition.

Some may think they are worshiping in the name of Jesus, but they are not necessarily worshiping in the nature of Jesus. *Name* and *nature* are one in the Bible. It is impossible to divide Jesus between name and nature. When we ask anything in the name of Jesus, it does not mean pronouncing the name "Jesus." It means that we are in conformity to His nature. To chant the name "Jesus" has no power in it. Whoever asks after His nature and asks in accordance to His Word, that man can get what he wants.

I cannot live contrary to the nature of Jesus on Monday and then Monday night when I face a crisis and I get on my knees and call on the name of Jesus and think that there is some magic in that name. I would be disappointed and disillusioned; for if I am not living in that name, I cannot pray properly in that name. If I am not living in that nature, I cannot pray rightfully in that nature. We cannot live after our nature and worship after His. When His nature and ours begin to harmonize under the influence of the Holy Spirit, the power of His name begins to be felt.

The Bible clearly teaches, "But we have the mind of Christ" (1 Cor. 2:16). Then Paul says, "To whom God would make known what is the riches of the glory of this mystery among the Gentiles; which is Christ in you, the hope of glory" (Col. 1:27).

The same mystery that united Jesus with God also unites us with Jesus.

Worship in Whatever You Do

I know that the name of Jesus is far above all the names of all kings and queens and archangels and presidents and prime ministers. Above Moses, Aaron and all that have ever had honor in the entire world. I know that at the "name of Jesus every knee should bow, . . . and that every tongue confess that Jesus Christ is Lord, to the glory of God the Father" (Phil. 2:10-11). And that He will ride down the sky and He will call to the nations of the earth, and they will come before Him and He will be their judge supreme. I also know that we cannot take advantage of that name by any twisted religious magic. We have to live in that name; and you cannot rest until every area in your life rests in God, and everything honors God.

Does your business honor God? Are you living it yourself? If it does not honor God, then I cannot see you living for God and honoring Him. If your business does not honor God, you cannot honor God. You are buying and selling. You cut corners, you push and scream, and you cannot possibly please God.

What about your relation to the opposite sex? How can we worship God if our relation to the opposite sex is such that God is displeased? I am not a prude, but I believe that our relation with each other ought to be right and pure in every way.

I wonder about the relationships in your home life and your school life and your use of money and time. Is all this pleasing to God? Some imagine their time is their own and they can do with it as they please. Your time is not your own; it belongs to the God who created time.

If God gives you a few more years, remember, it is not yours. Your time must honor God, your home must honor God, your activity must honor God, and everything about you must honor God.

If you want to die right, then you have to live right; and if you want to be right when you are old, then you have to be right when you are young.

You are not worshiping right in any place until you are worshiping God right in every place. If you cannot worship Him in the kitchen, then you cannot worship Him audibly in the church.

How utterly terrible is the current idea that Christians can serve God at their own convenience. Do we seem to be the follower of the One who had nowhere to lay His head until He laid it back against the cross and died? So we need that time for preparation, testing and choosing. Thank God, there is time; I do not know when time will be called on us one of these days, but there is time now.

Worship is not a spotlight focusing on one area of life. True worship, worship that is pleasing to God, radiates throughout a person's entire life.

Prayer

Oh, God, we humble ourselves before that Mystery uniting us with Thee. We worship Thee not according to our understanding, which is inadequate, but we worship Thee in Spirit and truth. We honor Thee within our hearts, bow before that sacred burning bush and hide our faces in reverential fear.
In Jesus' name, amen.

The Natural Dwelling Place of God

But the hour cometh, and now is, when the true worshippers
shall worship the Father in spirit and in truth: for the
Father seeketh such to worship him.

JOHN 4:23

True worship accords with the nature of God. By that I mean we worship God according to what God is, and not according to what He is not. The frightful error of idolatry, and the reason God hates it so, is because it is worship according to what God is not. He said about the Samaritans, "You do not know what you worship; you worship according to what God is not. We Jews know what we worship" (see John 4:22). Salvation was of the Jews not because they were better than other people, because they were not. Their prophets said distinctly that they were worse than some people were, but God chose to reveal the truth to them and gave them the oracles. By such revelation, God made it possible for Israel to worship according to the nature of God. And Jesus Christ our Lord says that God is Spirit, and we worship according to that nature of God.

In light of this, we must keep in mind that God is not affected by the attributes of matter—He is not affected by weight, size or space. A well-taught Christian knows that the great God is not affected by space and that He contains space in His bosom. The well-instructed Christian knows that God is not affected by speed. God gets around all points. God is Spirit; God is not affected by location, and He is not in some place to which you come and recede; but God is all about us and contains space, and so He is not nearer to one place than He is to another. It is a great comfort to know that God is as near to one place as He is to another place.

Because God made us in His image, there is a part of us that is like God. The human soul is most like God of anything that has ever been created, and uniquely corresponds to God.

How can this be? There is so much sin in the world and so much that seems so ungodly. The simple answer is sin. Because man has fallen does not mean that which is fallen doesn't have about it yet the luminance of the likeness of God. It is easy for God to restore us and redeem us, because God has material to work with once made in His image.

Let us bring in an Old Testament illustration. Suppose a potter is making a beautiful clay pot. While spinning on the wheel, it runs into some sand or grit and falls apart. There it is now, broken and no longer useful. But the material out of which it is made, while it doesn't look like a teapot anymore, and there is no artistry there, and while the soul of the artist is not in it and cannot be in it because it has been broken on the wheel, still it is a simple matter for the potter to take up that material again, take out the offending parts and make it into another vessel. He could not do that if he had iron; he could not do it if he had rock; but he could do it with clay, because clay is the material with which he works. It was broken the first time, but he can restore it using the same material.

God made us in His image; and while we are not altogether clear about what that image of God is, we do know that the human soul relates to and responds to God. In the temptation in the Garden, man fell apart and lost the artistry, the beauty, the holiness of God. But he did not lose the potential to become godlike again if he got into the hands of the Divine Artist.

This is the purpose in redemption: taking on the material of fallen man and by the mystery of regeneration and sanctification, restoring it again so that he is like God and like Christ. This is why we preach redemption. That is what redemption is; it is not saving us from hell, although it does save us from hell; but more importantly, it is making it so that we can be like God again.

How does this take place?

Pray in the Spirit

First, nobody can worship without the Holy Ghost. God is Spirit; the Holy Spirit is the Spirit of God and, therefore, the Holy Spirit is the only one properly to lead the heart to worship God acceptably. The fallen human mind does not know how to worship God acceptably, so the Holy Spirit takes the fallen human mind, points it up, corrects it, purges it, aims it and directs it so that it is worshiping God. That is why it is so vastly and vitally important that we should know the Holy Spirit.

I have often felt like getting on my knees and apologizing to the Holy Spirit for the way the Church has treated Him. We have treated Him shoddily. We have treated Him in such a manner that if you were to treat a guest that way, the guest would slip away grief stricken and never return. We have treated the Holy Spirit wretchedly. He is God Himself, the link binding the Father and the Son, and is the substance uncreated, which is deity. Yet the Holy Spirit is typically ignored in the average church, even in the average gospel church.

If we have a doxology to begin the service, we sing, "Praise God from whom all blessings flow; Praise Him all creatures here below; Praise Him above ye heavenly host; Praise Father, Son and Holy Ghost." That is a mention of the Holy Spirit. And if we have a benediction at the close, we say, "The love of God the Father and the communion of the Holy Ghost." So we have the Holy Spirit again. We have Him at the opening of the service and at the closing of the service. Outside of that, we do not count on His presence. Talking about the Holy Spirit is not the same as honoring Him in our worship.

How many go to church on a Sunday, counting on the Holy Spirit being present? How many really count on the Holy Spirit speaking to them? How many trust the Holy Spirit to take on a human voice and speak through it? That He is going to take a human ear and listen through it?

The idea that anybody can offer worship is all wrong. The view that we can worship ignoring the Spirit is all wrong. To crowd the Spirit into a corner and ignore Him, quench Him, resist Him and yet worship God acceptably is a great heresy, which needs correcting. Only the Holy Spirit knows how to worship God acceptably.

In the book of Romans (8:26), you will find that only the Holy Spirit knows how to pray. "Likewise the Spirit also helpeth our infirmities: for we know not what we should pray for as we ought: but the Spirit itself maketh intercession for us with groanings which cannot be uttered. And he that searcheth the hearts knoweth what is the mind of the Spirit, because he maketh intercession for the saints according to the will of God" (vv. 26-27). In our prayers, there will be mutterings and repetition until the Holy Spirit takes them, purges them, cleanses them and makes them acceptable to God through Jesus Christ our Mediator.

Therefore, it is impossible to pray without the Spirit. The most powerful prayers are prayed in the Spirit, and we cannot worship without the Holy Spirit. Either we ignore Him or we exploit Him for our personal pleasure and entertainment. I think it is time we rethink this whole matter of the place of the Holy Spirit in the church of our Lord Jesus Christ. We should rethink it in the light of the Scriptures, because without the Holy Spirit, we are as Israel when she continued worshiping God after the fire left the holy place and there was no Shekinah, no glory, no fire, no light and no Presence there. Yet Israel continued to worship vainly and futilely. Pitifully, she continued to worship, forgetting that the Spirit of worship had left her long ago.

Spirituality is one of the ingredients of worship, and without spirituality, I cannot worship God in a way that is acceptable to Him, no matter how much I worship. If it is not acceptable worship, then it is vain worship and better not attempted.

Pray with Sincerity

The second ingredient in worship is sincerity as distinct from formality or duplicity. We have extreme and heinous examples of the latter from our missionaries. The missionaries tell us about the heathen who worshiped their god, and they liked to cheat him.

You do not have to go to some pagan society to see this. Some of us have become quite brazen in this. We make promises to God that we do not intend to keep, thinking we can get from God what we want. We think that we can cheat the Lord, and by crossing our fingers, the Lord will not hear, will not notice us.

We have to be absolutely sincere if we are going to worship God, which is distinct from formality. I do not know whether anything merely done formally has any meaning at all. It is possible to go to religious ritual and not even know what we are doing or why we are doing it; we're just going through meaningless motions and repeating empty words and phrases.

The Lord pointed to a little child and said that the little child was an example. I believe that one thing about a little child is complete sincerity. No matter how many embarrassing things he may be saying, a child is nevertheless absolutely sincere. And it is this sincerity that we must cultivate prayerfully if our worship is to be accepted of almighty God.

What a terrible thing to spend a lifetime making offerings to the Almighty, all of which are rejected. Cain made his offering to the Almighty, but God did not answer and would not accept it, and Cain's countenance fell.

Pray with Honesty

Honesty is the third ingredient. It must be in all our prayers distinct from mere propriety. I suppose honesty and sincerity are twin brothers and cannot be separated, although they are separate and not identical. But there must be complete honesty before God. If I get on my knees and pray, "Oh, Lord, meet our missionary budget," and then the Lord knows that I am not going to give anything toward it, He knows that I am praying dishonestly.

If I pray, "Oh, Lord, save this man," but I have never done anything toward winning him, I'm dishonest. If I ask God to do things that I could do for myself, I am dishonest in my praying. But we have glossed this over until it sounds shocking to hear it said. It is true nevertheless.

Pray with Simplicity

Fourth, we must have simplicity in worship as distinct from sophistry and sophistication.

I have heard a few people pray that were utterly simple, almost embarrassingly simple. They were so simple-hearted that you tended to feel perhaps that they were not intellectually strong. But there is no incompatibility between intellectual power and simplicity of heart. Jesus Christ our Lord was simple to the point of being direct in His relationships. To our old Quaker friends who lived generations ago, simplicity was everything to them.

When the old English Quakers went before the king, they would not take off their broad-rimmed hats because they thought that was giving too much honor to a man. They would do anything before God, but insisted on wearing those hats and looked out many a set of bars in many a prison just for that reason. Personally, I do not think there would be any harm in it; I would take my hat off. There is nothing wrong with uncovering your head. You are certainly not worshiping anybody; but the point is, they did what they believed and God honored them for living according to their faith. Simplicity, utter simplicity. They said "thee" and "thou" and they called each other Mary and John, whatever the name was, and they taught the church of Christ to be simple.

If we would ever break ourselves down and suddenly be faced with death or some other tragedy or terror, we would be forced to see how unnatural we are and how unlike ourselves. We have lived like zoo lions, utterly unlike the lions that roam the wilds of Africa; and so we are in this civilization of ours pressed on every side.

There must be simplicity before going to pray or worship God. You must worship God simply; and I do not care who you are or what you are, it must be simple.

It takes simplicity and humility to worship God acceptably. Most of us are a half dozen people. I have four or five reputations. To some people I am this; to some people I am that; and I suppose everyone else is the same. When we try to live up to our reputations, it is always difficult, and we always get into trouble.

Pray from the Heart

Then, true worship must be internal—internality as distinct from externalism. We ought to thank God from the depths of our heart that we do not need any machinery to worship God.

You can worship God in spirit and in truth through the depths of your own heart as well as the angels in glory can worship God. You do not have to have anything; you do not have to die with a crucifix in your hand, or any other religious artifact.

Anything may mean something to a worshiping heart, and it can mean nothing if the heart is not worshiping. A wedding ring may mean a great deal to a woman, but only because she believes it tells her something about a man, not because it has any intrinsic value. If she loses it down the sink, she will sorrow a little, but she will not lose her husband, she will not lose his love and she will not lose that for which it stood. She can get another ring. Therefore, worship is an internal thing.

My personal worship tells something about God and me. I can worship truly, because something is true between God and me. If after years of going to the same church, I come to associate that church with worshiping God, that is natural, that is psychological, that is a conditional reflex; I think they call it that in psychology. But it does not mean that if I do not go to that church again, or the church burns down, that I cannot worship God.

I believe it is time that illuminating persons begin the arduous task of reforming Christian worship. And as we begin to understand it again in the church of Christ, I believe it will bring revival to us.

Back to our basic text: "Who is thy Lord, worship thou Him, so that He shall greatly desire thy beauty."

The soul is a God-shaped void. If I would carry it further, I would say your soul is a God-shaped garment, like a glove shaped to fit your hand. God cannot enter, because it is full of rubbish. Try putting a lot of junk in the glove sometime and then try placing your hand into it; you cannot do it. That glove must be empty before a hand can go into it.

The heart must be empty before God can enter. That is why at the altars, in times of evangelism and prayer and the pressure to get people right with God, we insist on an emptying out of ourselves. Your soul is a God-shaped garment, and God wants to clothe Himself with it. But He cannot enter because there is rubbish in it. Search your heart and find out how much rubbish you have collected over the past years. How much moral rubbish, how much intellectual rubbish, how much rubbish of habit, of custom, of things you do and do not do, think and do not think. We must empty it all out.

I would like to say that I have found some new way, but there is no new way. Empty the rubbish out of your soul, turn yourself up to God in the name of the Lord Jesus Christ and He will fill you, come in and clothe Himself with you. God will not wear an unclean garment. God wants to wear a pure garment.

Once we have emptied ourselves of everything, we must be cleansed. Only through the blood of the Lamb can that emptied soul be cleansed so that God can enter. An emptied and cleansed soul is the natural dwelling place of God. So let us ask God to cleanse us. We can empty ourselves but we can never cleanse ourselves.

If you have something in you preventing God from entering, you can empty that out. But if after you empty, you are still unclean, you can never cleanse yourself. Only God can do that by the blood of the everlasting covenant, by the fire of the Holy Ghost and by the discipline of obedience. God cleanses

His people and makes them white and pure in the blood of the Lamb.

Everyone who knows about birds knows there is what is called natural habitats. You do not go to the swamp to find a wood thrush. If you want to hear a wood thrush, you go to the cool woods when the shadows fall. Go there and wait for the evening to come and then the wood thrush will come. Quietly at first, and then louder and bolder, and as the shadows grow deeper, she will play her lovely flute in the darkness. But she will never go to the swamp.

If you want to hear a red-winged blackbird make its clumping sound, you do not go to the cool woods in the evening; you go to the swampy land where the cattails slip their brown flowers up. There you will find the red-winged blackbird. If you want to hear a wren sing, you do not go to the woods, and you do not go to the swamp; you go to your own backyard and there she will be with delight. It is what they call natural habitat.

I believe that the Holy Spirit has a natural habitat. By habitat, I mean He makes Himself at home, heard or felt; it is where He can speak and where He can live. That natural habitat is nothing else but the soul of a man or woman.

You ask how such a thing can be. Because God made that soul in the image of God, and God can dwell in His own image without embarrassment. And just as the blackbird can sing among the cattails, and just as the rabbit can hop among the briars, and just as the wood thrush can sing unseen at the edge of the woods at night, so the Holy Spirit wants to come into your soul and live in it. Not weekending there, not a houseguest for a while, but making your soul a permanent habitation.

Only sin can prevent that, which is why worship and sin are incompatible. That is why you cannot deal with the matter of true worship and omit the question of sin. Sin can prevent worship. You cannot worship God with unconfessed sin reigning in your heart. "Behold, I stand at the door, and knock: if any man hear my voice, and open the door, I will come in to him, and will sup with him, and he with me" (Rev. 3:20). Here is the picture of Jesus in your house, dwelling with you. "I will come in, unto you. I will take you unto me, but I will come in unto you." Jesus desires to be in the house of His friend—in your house.

Your soul is a God-shaped glove. God wants to enter into it, but it is full of rubbish. Get rid of the rubbish and you will not have to beg God to come in.

The old-fashioned light bulb was made in such a way that at the end of it was a little projection. When pumped empty, it became a vacuum. As a kid, I used to take a pair of pliers and break that little projection off, and there was a popping sound as 14 pounds per square inch of atmospheric pressure rushed into that bulb. You did not have to get in the bulb and get on your knees, beg and say, "Please come, atmosphere, please come in." All you had to do was take away the obstruction and the atmosphere rushed in. Nature abhors a vacuum.

The human soul is a vacuum, and we have filled it with trash. As far as God is concerned, we only have to empty it and God rushes in, cleanses it and fills it. Not for us, but for Himself; and He does not have to be begged. The most natural thing in the universe is for the Creator to indwell the soul of man.

The Home
by Gerhard Tersteegen (1697-1769)

Thou who givest of Thy gladness
Till the cup runs o'er—
Cup whereof the pilgrim weary
Drinks to thirst no more
Not a-nigh me, but within me
Is Thy joy divine;
Thou, O Lord, hast made Thy dwelling
In this heart of mine.

Prayer

*Eternal God, who dwells in the heavens above us, we humbly
bow before Thee with anxious thoughts of fellowship with
Thee. We thank Thee that Thou hast been enough for us. Our
thirsty hearts have been satiated in Thee. Amen.*

The Absolute Worthship of Christ

I charge you, O daughters of Jerusalem, if ye find my beloved, that ye tell him, that I am sick of love. What is thy beloved more than another beloved, O thou fairest among women? what is thy beloved more than another beloved, that thou dost so charge us? My beloved is white and ruddy, the chiefest among ten thousand. His head is as the most fine gold, his locks are bushy, and black as a raven. His eyes are as the eyes of doves by the rivers of waters, washed with milk, and fitly set. His cheeks are as a bed of spices, as sweet flowers: his lips like lilies, dropping sweet smelling myrrh. His hands are as gold rings set with the beryl: his belly is as bright ivory overlaid with sapphires. His legs are as pillars of marble, set upon sockets of fine gold: his countenance is as Lebanon, excellent as the cedars. His mouth is most sweet: yea, he is altogether lovely. This is my beloved, and this is my friend, O daughters of Jerusalem.

Song of Songs 5:8-16

This passage in Song of Songs is a parable of our relationship with this one called the Shepherd. It details the marvelous details of that relationship. Our Lord is the Shepherd; the Redeemed Church is the fair bride. In an hour of distress, this

Bride tells the daughters of Jerusalem among whom she lives, "If you find my beloved tell him that I am sick with love." Naturally, they inquire, "What is your beloved more than another beloved that thou doest so charge us?"

It is a legitimate question, and the world has a perfect right to ask it of the Church. If the Church insists that the Lord is worthy and a worthy lover, then the world has a right to ask what kind of lover He is. Why should we be promoting Him, "what is thy beloved more than another beloved?"

Others are offered up for the world's admiration and worship, so why this One? What qualities recommend him to them?

Lord of All

In the book of Psalms, David talks about this. "My heart is indicting a good matter: I speak of the things, which I have made touching the king: my tongue is the pen of a ready writer. Thou art fairer than the children of men: grace is poured forth by thy lips . . . all thy garments smell of myrrh, and aloes, and cassia, out of the ivory palaces, whereby they have made thee glad" (Ps. 45:1-2,8). This psalm is a rapt description of this shepherd king wooing the young bride to himself. Ask Peter that question and he would say, "He is Lord of all."

The entire purpose and focus of our worship is none other than the Lord Himself, our righteousness, the Lord Jesus Christ. He is the Lord of all, and in order that we might get it before us, we need to know what He is Lord of and why we should love Him.

This is a fair consideration. Why is He more than any other man? Furthermore, why should we worship him? We can worship Jesus Christ the man without idolatry because He is also God. By the mystery of the theanthropic union, He has united humanity to deity. Jesus Christ is both divine and human in nature and has taken humanity up into God so that He Himself is God. He has joined in the beauty and wonder of the theanthropic union of God and man in one so that whatever God is, Christ is as well. Therefore, Jesus could truthfully say, "He that hath seen me has seen the Father" (John 14:9).

Our confidence is that when we worship the Lord Jesus, we are not displeasing the Father, for we are worshiping the Father in Him. This is the mystery of the hypostatic union, joining us forever to God through the Lord Jesus Christ.

I will divide it a little bit so that we can understand it better. Let me begin with a marvelous hymn by Oliver Wendell Holmes (1809–1894):

> LORD of all being, throned afar,
> Thy glory flames from sun and star;
> Centre and soul of every sphere,
> Yet to each loving heart how near!

The hymn writer did not say "He is the Lord of all beings" but that He is the "Lord of all being," which is something else, and something more. He is the Lord of all actual existence. He is the Lord of all kinds of beings—the Lord of all spiritual being and all natural being and all physical being. He is the Lord of all being, and when we worship Him, we encompass all being.

Some give themselves up to the disciplines of science, technology, philosophy, art and music. When we worship the Lord

Jesus Christ, we embrace and encompass all disciplines, because He is the Lord of them all. Therefore, He is the Lord of all being, and the enemy of all not being. He is the Lord of all life.

These are fundamental to any right understanding that Jesus Christ is the Lord of all life: "For the life was manifested, and we have seen it, and bear witness, and show unto you that eternal life, which was with the Father, and was manifested unto us" (1 John 1:2).

Charles Wesley understood this and put it in his immortal hymn, "Jesus, Lover of My Soul."

> Plenteous grace with thee is found,
> grace to cover all my sin;
> let the healing streams abound,
> make and keep me pure within.
> Thou of life the fountain art,
> freely let me take of thee;
> spring thou up within my heart . . .

Lord of Creation

He is the Lord of all kinds of life, so He is the Lord of all essential possibilities of life.

All of creation is populated with many kinds of life. In the spring, the buds will come out, promising floral life all over. He is the Lord of that kind of life. Spring will bring back the birds, the rabbits will be out, and you will see the animals. That is another kind of life, and He is the Lord of that kind as well.

Then we have intellectual life: the life of imagination and reason. He is the Lord of that kind of life.

And we have the spiritual life, and He is the Lord of that kind of life. He is the Lord of angels, and He is the Lord of the cherubim and seraphim. So He is the Lord of all life, and He is the Lord of all sorts of life.

So, in response to the inquiry, "What is thy beloved more than another beloved?" We can say with confidence, "He is Lord of all."

Lord of Wisdom

Further, the Holy Spirit says, "He is the Lord of all wisdom." All eternal wisdom lies in Jesus Christ as a treasure hidden away, and no wisdom exists outside of Him. All the eternal purposes of God are in Him, because His perfect wisdom enables Him to plan ahead. All history is the slow development of His purposes.

This is difficult to justify in light of the world around us. Today all we see are the laborers in creation at work. We see the laborers working on the external scaffoldings, and things do not look very beautiful now. Any building in the stage of construction will not possess the beauty of its finished state.

Whether they know it or not, these laborers are doing the will of God and are bringing things about. The individual workers may not have the finished picture in mind, only the small area they are working on at the time; however, they are moving the project to its final state of completion, fulfilling the will of the general contractor. Even the devil unwittingly fulfills God's will. God is making all evil men as well as all good men; and all adverse things as well as all favorable things work for a bringing forth of His glory in the day when all shall be fulfilled in Him (see Rom. 8:28).

Lord of Righteousness

Then, He is the Lord of all righteousness and all concepts of righteousness and all possibilities of righteousness. He is wisdom and righteousness, and there is no getting around Him. No book you can read on Christian ethics or any other kind of ethics can tell you anything He does not already know and that He is not already Lord of. It is written, "But unto the Son He said, 'Thy throne, O God, is for ever and ever, a sceptre of thy kingdom is a right sceptre. Thou lovest righteousness and hatest wickedness: therefore God, thy God, hath anointed thee with the oil of gladness above thy fellows'" (Ps. 445:6-7).

When the Old Testament High Priest went into the holy of holies to offer sacrifices once a year, he wore a miter on his forehead. On that miter were engraved in Hebrew the words "holiness unto the Lord." This Jesus Christ our Lord and High Priest is righteous, and He is the Lord of Righteousness.

He is also the Lord of all mercy, for He establishes His kingdom upon rebels.

First, He has to redeem them, win them and renew a right spirit within them; and all this He does. He is the Lord of all mercy, He is the Lord of all power and He transforms these rebels according to His righteousness.

Lord of Moral Beauty

God put something in the human breast making it capable of understanding and appreciating beauty. He put in us the love of harmonious forms, the love of and appreciation for color and beautiful sounds. It is in everyone. He put in us also the love of moral forms of line and color. All things that are beautiful to the eye and the ear are only the external counterparts of that internal beauty, which is moral beauty.

It was said of Jesus Christ our Lord that there was no beauty in Him that we should desire Him. Artists have painted Jesus with a tender feminine face and clear beautiful eyes and an open delightful countenance, and with curly hair streaming down His shoulders. They have completely forgotten that the Bible declares that there was no beauty in Him that we should desire Him.

They had forgotten that when the high priest would crucify Jesus, they had to make an arrangement to identify Him. Judas Iscariot did not say, "When we get there, pick out that beautiful one with a feminine face, curls down His back and the light on His face; He is the one." They were standing there with their typical Jewish haircuts and Hebrew garments, all looking alike, so Judas had to give the soldiers a signal. "The one I kiss, that will be the one." They did not recognize Jesus. When Jesus came, Judas passed by Peter, John, Philip and the rich man, kissed Jesus, and said, "That's the man there."

If Jesus had looked as beautiful physically as they paint Him, why would it be necessary that He had to be betrayed with a kiss? He simply did not look like that; there was no beauty in Him that we should desire Him.

The beauty of Jesus that has charmed the centuries is this moral beauty of which even His enemies acknowledge. Friedrich Nietzsche, the great German philosopher, perhaps the greatest nihilist and one of the greatest antichrists that ever lived in the world, died beating his forehead on the floor of his cell. He once said, "That man Jesus I love, but I don't like

Paul." He did not like theology, and he did not like to hear how you have to be saved and about the necessity of the new birth. In particular, he objected to justification by faith. However, there was something attractive about Jesus that he could not help but love.

So there is moral beauty in the Lord Jesus Christ, and He is the Lord of all beauty of moral form and moral texture. He is the Lord of it all.

Halfway Between Heaven and Hell

Sin has scarred the world and made it inharmonious, unsymmetrical and has filled hell with ugliness. If you love beautiful things, you had better stay out of hell, for hell will be the quintessence of all that is morally ugly. The spirit of things determines the external manifestation of that spirit, and I believe hell will be the ugliest place in all God's creation. When rough men say something is as "ugly as hell," they are using a proper and valid comparison.

Heaven is the place of harmonious numbers. Heaven is the place of loveliness; the place of beauty, because the One who is all beautiful is there. He is the Lord of all beauty, and earth lies between all that is ugly in hell and all that is beautiful in heaven. Earth lies between it, and you see the ugliness set over against the beauty.

Why is it like that? Why is there light and shadows? Why is there ugliness and beauty? Why are there so much good and so much bad? Why is there that which is pleasant and that which is tragic and hard to live with? It is because the earth lies halfway between heaven's beauty and hell's ugliness.

You say, "Why are people capable of doing what they do?" The answer is because they lie halfway between heaven and hell.

The Lord of All and His Bride

Is there any Christian who has not been hurt by some other Christian, and maybe a real Christian too? Why is it that a man will be on his knees praying earnestly one day and another day he will hurt another Christian? Because we stand halfway between heaven and hell. You and I must be pulled out of all this. The Lord of beauty is saving His people from the ugliness of sin.

Our Lord Jesus Christ came into the world that He might save us from the ugliness of sin to a beautiful heaven.

The Old Testament gives us the story of a man named Isaac. His father, Abraham, called for his servant to go find an acceptable bride for his son (see Gen. 24). With the help of the Holy Spirit, that old servant went down into the town Abraham indicated and found a young woman there. The Bible pictures her as being very beautiful. Her name was Rebekkah and she must have been beautiful, because the servant was instructed to find a bride that was beautiful to look upon.

Isaac is a type of our Lord Jesus Christ. God the Father sent the Holy Spirit out among the people of the world to win a bride for Christ, one that was worthy of Him. The bride's significance was to rest in the groom. She has no worth of her own, but her worth lies in her relationship to the groom. Jesus Christ is the groom and is worthy of our love, adoration and joyful worship.

Rebekkah was merely the daughter of her father. But, when she was taken to Isaac, she took on a new identity—the identify of her groom. Our identity is now in our Groom. The past identity is forgotten, with all its obligations. Our Groom is now our identity, and nothing in our past matters anymore. The bride not only takes on the identity of the groom but also his name as well. She is now forever known by that name.

This Groom Shepherd is worthy of our affection and is deserving of us leaving everything behind and embracing Him as our own.

Prayer

Oh God, in great humility we bow before Thee and take upon ourselves Thy name and Thy nature. Everything in our past is lost in glorious oblivion, and all our future is wrapped up in Thee. We accept Thee as our Groom Shepherd and are eternally grateful that the gracious Spirit of God sought us out and brought us unto Thee. We long for nothing else but Thee.
Amen.

THE AUTHENTICITY OF OWNERSHIP

But unto the Son he saith, Thy throne, O God, is for ever and ever:
a sceptre of righteousness is the sceptre of thy kingdom. Thou hast loved
righteousness, and hated iniquity; therefore God, even thy God, hath
anointed thee with the oil of gladness above thy fellows.

HEBREWS 1:8-9

During the first few years of my ministry, if I could not have prayed and asked God for things, I would have starved to death, dragging my wife and family down with me. So I believe in praying for things. I believe that we can claim the promises of God to supply our daily needs. But that is not all there is to Christianity, and it certainly represents the lowest section of it. Too many people are all possessed with the idea of getting things from God to the extent of obscuring everything else.

There is so much more in the Christian life than getting things from God. Our personal relationship to Jesus Christ is the most important thing about us, which is defined for us in the worship we offer to God. The important thing is the object of our worship; and for the Christian, that is none other than

God, the Father of our Lord Jesus Christ. Because of the crucial aspect of this, we must know who it is we worship.

The Scriptures teach us that He is the Lord of all wisdom and He is the Lord of the Father of the everlasting ages. Not the "everlasting Father" as it says in our *King James Version*, but the "Father of the everlasting ages." This Father lays out the ages as an architect would lay out his blueprint or as a real estate developer lays out a small town and then builds hundreds of houses on it. But God is not dealing with buildings and local developments. He is dealing with the ages and is the Lord of all wisdom. Because He is perfect in wisdom, He is able to do this, and history is but the slow development of His purposes.

A Plan for the Ages

Take a house that is being built; the architect has drawn it down to the last tiny dot and X. He knows everything about it, has studied it thoroughly and writes his name at the bottom. The plans are now complete, and he turns it over to the contractor who farms it out to the electrician and plumber and all the rest. The building process begins. In the beginning, it does not look too encouraging. Visit the site and you will wonder what it is going to be. It doesn't look like anything at the moment. It is a mess now, with a steam shovel's great ugly nose digging out a hole and throwing it up on the bank or into trucks to haul away. In another place trucks are unloading bricks, and everything seems to be a confused conglomeration of this and that.

Come back six, eight, ten months later, and you see a charming house there with no signs of the construction confusion. The landscapers have been in, and the evergreen trees are standing there with their little green spikes by the windows, and it is a beautiful thing.

Order Out of the Chaos

We now are to believe that the Father of the everlasting ages, the Lord of all wisdom, has laid out His plan and is working toward a predetermined goal. All we see now is a church all mixed up and sore, distressed by schisms, and rent asunder by heresies. We see her backslidden in one part of the world, in confusion in another part, and we shrug our shoulders and wonder, What is all this, and who is behind all this? The answer is, He is the Lord of the ages; He is laying it all out, and what you are seeing now is only the steam shovel working, the truck backed up with bricks, that is all. You can only see workers in overalls going about killing time. You are just seeing people, and people make you sick because of the way we do, the way we are. To the uninitiated, everything looks like confusion and turmoil, as though no one was in charge.

We backslide and tumble around and are mixed up and run after will-o'-the-wisp and think it is the Shekinah glory. We hear an owl hoot and think it is the silver trumpet, and we take off in the wrong direction and spend a century catching up on ourselves. Return in another millennium or so and see what the Lord of all wisdom has done with it. No matter how much of a mess it appears, God has a way of working everything out for His glory. He is the Lord of all wisdom, and history is but the slow development of His purposes.

I am glad I am attached to something good, that there is something good somewhere in the universe. Despite appearances, behind all the mess of our world is the Lord of all wisdom sorting it out in His way and in His time.

I could not possibly be a Pollyanna optimist. I was born wrong. I would have to have had a different father and mother and a different ancestral line back at least 10 generations for me to have been a Pollyanna plum-pudding philosopher believing that everything was good. I cannot believe that. I do not think it is true. There is so much that is not right—everywhere. We might as well admit it. Wickedness prevails on so many fronts that it would be impossible to ignore it.

Some religious people try to black out all the negative and concentrate on the positive. If you want to get ahead in life, so they advise, ignore the negatives in your life and focus on the positive; and in the end, the positive will override all negative.

But, if you take the Bible as your guide, righteousness is not found among us. If you think it is, get on a bus somewhere when there's a crowd and you'll find that no matter how old and feeble you are, you will get the rib or two, or at least badly dinged by the elbow of some housewife on her way home. It is hard to concentrate on the positive with a sharp elbow in your side. And people are just not good. Among the first things we learn to do is something bad and something mean. The first word a baby learns to say is "no." Sin is everywhere.

Turn on the radio and try to get something educational or cultural and all you hear are songs about automobiles and cigarettes and sex. If it were not for the bad news on radio, the airwaves would be gloriously silent. It is not a good world we live in. You can become a Protestant, but that does not help much. You can be an American boasting in all your Bill of Rights guaranteed in the Constitution, and that does not help too much either.

Righting All That Is Wrong

However, when you attach yourself to the Lord of Glory, you are connected with something righteous. He is righteousness itself, and all of the possibility of righteousness is summed up in Him. "But unto the Son he saith, Thy throne, O God, is for ever and ever: a sceptre of righteousness is the sceptre of thy kingdom. Thou hast loved righteousness, and hated iniquity; therefore God, even thy God, hath anointed thee with the oil of gladness above thy fellows" (Heb. 1:8-9).

In this mixed-up, confused world, we need not despair, for we have a perfectly righteous Savior. He proved Himself with life among the people of His day. During His earthly life and ministry, His enemies spied on Him, sending people to search into His life to trip Him in something. Can you imagine if Jesus had made a mistake anywhere or lost His temper even once? All the sharp beady eyes of hell were following Him, trying to catch something out of His mouth. When the end of His days had almost come, He turned on them and said, "Which one of you convicts me of sin?" Nobody answered.

Sometime, I want to preach a sermon on mercy; I do not think I ever have. Of course, I have woven it into all of my preaching, but never just on the mercy of the Lord Jesus Christ. Our Lord sees how bad we are, but He is the Lord of all mercy and He does not care. In His great kindness, He takes rebels and unrighteous persons, sinners, and makes them His own and establishes them in righteousness and renews a right spirit within them. His righteousness becomes their righteousness, and out of chaos comes the divine order. This is the church, a company of believers, and together He is their Lord. He is the Lord of all power.

In the New Testament, we have a counterpart to the Song of Songs:

> And after these things I heard a great voice of much people in heaven, saying, Alleluia; Salvation, and glory, and honour, and power, unto the Lord our God: For true and righteous are his judgments: for he hath judged the great whore, which did corrupt the earth with her fornication, and hath avenged the blood of his servants at her hand. Again, they said, Alleluia. And her smoke rose up for ever and ever. And the four and twenty elders and the four beasts fell down and worshipped God that sat on the throne, saying, Amen; Alleluia. And a voice came out of the throne, saying, Praise our God, all ye his servants, and ye that fear him, both small and great (Rev. 19:1-5).

This is not hysteria, but ecstasy; there is a difference. Hysteria is based on emotion manipulated by exterior stimulus; but ecstasy is based upon mystery illuminating in the interior part of man's nature. This was ecstasy. It would be worthwhile to be put in a salt mine on the Isle of Patmos to have a vision like that.

Redeeming All That Is Lost

Years ago, I read one of the greatest books ever written of its kind, *Les Misérables* by Victor Hugo. In it, there was one of the tenderest and pathetic passages I think I have ever read in all literature.

You would have to go to the Bible to find things as deeply moving. Here was the story of a young man, one of the upper class of nobles, and the noble woman he was in love with. Then there was a pale face, a little urchin girl from the streets of Paris, dressed in poor rags, with a pale, tubercular face. She also loved the nobleman but did not dare say so. The young nobleman used the young girl to carry notes back and forth to his fiancée and never dreamed this poor sallow-faced girl dressed in rags had lost her heart to him and his nobility. When he discovered this, he went to find her and see what he could do to help her and found her lying on the bed of rags in the tenement house in the low section of Paris.

This time she cannot get up to greet him or carry a note to his fiancée. He says to her, "What can I do for you?"

She tells him, "I'm dying; I'll be gone in a moment."

"What can I do? Tell me, anything."

And she said, "Would you do one thing for me before I close my eyes for the last time? Would you, when I am dead, kiss my forehead?"

I know it was only Victor Hugo's brilliant imagination, but he had seen that in Paris. He had gone through the sewers, had seen this and knew about it. Hugo knew that you could beat a girl down, clothe her in rags, fill her with tuberculosis and make her so thin that the wind would blow her off course when she walked down a dirty street. But you could not take out of her heart that thing that makes her want to love a man.

God told Adam, "And the LORD God said, It is not good that the man should be alone; I will make him an help meet for him" (Gen. 2:18). And God made a woman to be a helpmeet for man;

you cannot take that out of human nature. Victor Hugo knew it when he wrote his classic novel. In human nature is planted the desire and need to love.

Our Lord Jesus Christ came down and found the human race like that: consumptive, wan, pale-faced and dying, and He took on Himself all her death and rose the third day and took all the pathos out and all of the pity out. Now she comes leaning on the arm of her beloved. She comes walking into the presence of God, and He presents her not as a poor pitiful wretch whose forehead He kissed when she was dead, but as His happy bright-eyed bride, to be partaker with all the saints, worthy to stand beside Him and be His bride in the glory. What is her authority, what is her right and by what authority does she walk into the presence of God?

We have an Old Testament illustration of this. Abraham sent his trusted servant to go and bring back a bride for his son Isaac. This servant was authorized to bestow upon her jewelry as a token from her groom. It was a symbol of his acceptance of the bride. Now, how was Isaac going to know his bride? What would set her apart from all others? He was going to know her by the jewelry that she had on. He had sent it, and when she came back with it, he would recognize her by his jewelry she wore. And so Scripture says that Isaac took Rebekkah and she became his bride.

The Lord of Glory sent the Holy Ghost at Pentecost to get a bride, and He will know her by the jewelry she wears.

And what is that jewelry?

For one, it is the fruit of the Spirit. Love, joy, peace, temperance, kindness, and all that. He will know her by what

He has bestowed upon her. Each of the fruit of the Spirit responds to the nature of Christ. He looks into our life, sees what He recognizes as coming from Him and accepts it.

Perhaps the biggest jewel will be that of worship—the bright, shiny, glorious spirit of worship that rests upon the bride of Christ. It is something that is implanted deep into the nature of man. Not all the depravity of human wickedness can destroy that impulse to reach out and up in worship. When God sees that worship, purified by the Spirit and the Blood, He responds and recognizes it as His.

Our Lord Jesus Christ will know His bride. He knows who you are, and He knows you by the jewelry He has given you. "He is thy Lord and he shall greatly desire thy beauty, worship thou Him."

The Irish hymn writer Jean Sophia Pigott (1845–1882) understood this and gave the world the essence of her joy in Christ.

Jesus, I am resting, resting,
In the joy of what Thou art;
I am finding out the greatness
Of thy loving heart.
Thou hast bid me gaze upon Thee,
And Thy beauty fills my soul,
For by Thy Transforming power
Thou hast made me whole.

These are the marks on us that authenticate our belonging to this "Lord of the Father of the everlasting ages."

Prayer

O God our Father, we thank Thee for Jesus Christ
Thy Son. We have not done anything that we can
think of but what we are ashamed. We have not done
anything but of what we ought to be ashamed. We have not
got anything—our brains, our bodies, our souls, our spirits,
we have not done anything ourselves—except what Thou
hast given us. What Thou hast given us we are not ashamed of.
We are glad for and deeply appreciative of Thy jewels that
adorn our life; these jewels that show the world whose we are.
In Jesus' name, amen.

The Lord of Our Worship

But ye are a chosen generation, a royal priesthood, an holy nation, a
peculiar people; that ye should shew forth the praises of him who hath
called you out of darkness into his marvellous light.

1 Peter 2:9

What is the purpose of the local church? And why is the church necessary?

According to the Bible, a local church exists to do corporately what each Christian should do individually all week: namely, worship God and show forth the excellencies of Him who has called us out of darkness into His marvelous light; reflect back the glory of Him who shined down on us, even God, even Christ, even the Holy Ghost. All that Christ has done for us in the past and all that He is doing now leads to this one end. This is not being taught very much today—that we are saved to worship God. We have it that we are saved for a number of reasons.

If you were to ask the average Christian why he was saved, he might respond by referring to peace of mind or being delivered from smoking. If he is a businessman, he might say he took the Lord Jesus as his helper because he was failing in business and wanted Him to be his business partner. We have many other reasons, and I am not going to be too hard on people. In the New Testament, people came to the Lord for many reasons. One man came because his boy was sick. A woman came because her daughter was sick. Another woman came because she had had a chronic disease for 12 years. A politician climbed a tree and looked down because his heart ached; and Nicodemus came by night to the Lord because his religion was not adequate and his heart was empty. Therefore, the Lord received them all, and the Lord receives everyone who comes to Him in faith today, even if their motives may not be the highest.

The point is, why should we always stay where we began? Why should the church be a spiritual school composed of first-graders who never go beyond the first grade? Nobody wants to get any further than this, and I do not mind saying that I am somewhat sick about it all. It seems to be an awful, mixed-up concept of Christianity.

The Lord Jesus Christ died on the cross that He might make His people worshipers of God. That is why we were born, that we might show forth the excellencies of Him who has called us out of darkness into His marvelous light. "He is thy Lord, worship thou Him." And we see that purpose—worship—when it is all over and the consummation has taken place and been fulfilled. The beasts, the elders and the creatures under the sea, above the earth, in the earth, and in the heavens are all crying aloud, "Holy, holy, holy to the Lord God Almighty, which was, and is, and is to come." The purpose of God is that He might redeem us, put us all in the heavenly choir and keep us there singing His praises and showing forth His excellencies while the ages roll. This is the purpose of God in redemption.

He has done it for us and is still doing now what He has done; everything leads to one end, and all we do should lead to one end. We must bring our ideas into harmony with the Lord of the Church. That means bringing your whole thought, your whole philosophy of Christianity, your whole conception of what the church is into harmony with the Lord of the Church and His teachings.

The Church's High Design

Religious people are a very noisy, wordy and active people. But activity for activity's sake is not of God. We might first clear away the idea that church is a social club. A church must have certain social commitments and certain fellowship, but we are not a social club. And we are not a current events forum. We often tend to read some magazine and then take off like an airplane off a ramp from what we've just read. So, we are not a current events forum and we are not a religious theater to provide a place for amateur entertainers to display their talent. We are none of these things.

We are a holy people, a royal priesthood, a holy generation called out of darkness to show forth the glory of the One who called us out. We should take whatever steps are needed to fulfill our high design as a New Testament church. To do less than this is to fail utterly, to fail God and to fail our Lord Jesus Christ who redeemed us. It is to fail ourselves and it is to fail our children. It is to fail the Holy Ghost who is come from the heart of Jesus to do in us a work. This work is to be done to make us a holy people, a sanctified people that are mirrors of the Almighty to reflect the glory of the most high God.

Why is this important? For the simple reason that if a local church in one generation fails of its high design of worship, the next generation in that church will depart from the faith altogether. That is how liberalism comes about. Many churches stand as a monument that the generation before failed God, and as a result the present generation succumbs to liberalism and does not preach the Word of God at all. With no Spirit of God upon them and no fire-baptized leaders, they need to compensate. Therefore, they keep it up by social activities and by tying into whatever is going on in the world. But as a church, it has failed and is not a church anymore. The glory has departed.

If we could see the visible cloud hanging over churches, the cloud that once hung over the camp of Israel in the wilderness, we could easily identify those churches acting in accord with their spiritual nature. If we were permitted to see the fire by night and the cloud by day, visibly hanging as a plume over the churches in which God is pleased, I wonder how many churches we would see testifying to all the world that this is God's dwelling place? Instead of that, we would see only monuments out in the country.

The church must not be accepted as it is or as we find it. We must check it with the Word of God and see if this is the way it should be. Then reverently and quietly, slowly but surely, patiently and lovingly bring the church into line with the New Testament to see if this is the way it would be done if the Holy Ghost were pleased. And when that takes place, the Holy Ghost begins to glow like lights in the church, and that is what my heart longs to see.

Live for the Purpose You Were Created

For individual professed Christians, if we fail the purpose for which God created us, then we had better never have been born.

How utterly and unspeakably tragic to be forever a broken vase. How utterly tragic that God should make me to be a vase in which He would place the flowers of paradise, the lily of the valley and the rose of Sharon, and out from that simple earthly vessel there would go forth a fragrance that would fill the universe of God. Then I allow that vase to be shattered on the floor, and it cannot be used for the purpose God had intended.

How utterly tragic to be a stringless harp and to have all the shape, outline and form of a Christian but have no strings that the Holy Ghost could play over.

How utterly terrible to be a barren fig tree, with nothing but leaves and no fruit!

Jesus walked out from Jerusalem with His people and saw a fig tree; it had leaves on it, and He went to that tree and found that it had no figs. The way a fig tree grows is the fruit comes first and then the leaves. When the leaves appear on the landscape, they tell everybody, "Come, there's fruit here"; and according to the nature of the tree, the fruit should have been there before the leaves. But in this case, the leaves were there and the order had been reversed; and when Jesus came, parted the leaves and reached in for figs, and there were no figs, He turned to His disciples and told them to look at that tree. There would be no more fruit forever, and He cursed it, and it withered from the top down.

What could be more terrible then a barren fig tree, to have the form and delineation of the Christian, but have no fruit. To be a star that shines not. To be those solemn, awful men in 2 Peter and Jude in his little epistle. Think about the dark stars that shine not and clouds without rain. How terrible to be a shattered mirror of the Almighty, meant of God to catch and reflect the beautiful light of God back to the entire universe. But instead is a cracked and shattered mirror that can reflect nothing, and thus is disapproved of God and banished from the garden; how terrible to be eternally aware of all this.

The frightful thing about human beings is our consciousness—that we are aware of things. If it was not for our awareness, nothing could harm us.

The rich man who died and found himself in hell was conscious he was there and knew his brothers were not there but would be coming soon. Hell would not be hell if it were not for the consciousness of it. If men slept comatose in hell, it could never be hell.

In the realm of psychology and psychiatry these days the devil is very busy, and has many men who can use phrases they have borrowed from Freud and the rest of them, telling us that we ought not to allow the consciousness of guilt to get us down because that is a guilt complex. We ought not to be too much bothered by religion.

One of the great heads of a great mental institution, after he had been long years head of that institution, was told, "Well, doctor, I suppose an awful lot of your patients in here have gone crazy over religion." He said, "To the best of my knowledge, in all the years that I have been head of this institution, I have never known one patient that came here because of religion; but I have known hundreds that came here that could have been saved from here by religion."

You ought to thank God if you have a care. I would not take that care away from you at all.

You have to be a purified people if you are going to be a worshiper of God, reflecting the image of Him that created you. But broken vessels, stringless harps, barren fig trees, clouds without water, cracked mirrors—how tragic and terrible it is.

You must be a purified people and be born into the world, unable to go back and cancel out your being, and yet before God be a broken vase. Before God be a life that does not shine. Before God be a harp that does not play, a tongue that does not bear fruit, failing God.

If you had teeth that were desperately in need of attention, the first thing you ought to do when you could afford to take a day off from work is attend to them. How much more important it is that I should find the blood that cleanses me from sin. Nothing should be permitted to hinder me. Friendships, they mean nothing. Business, better to sell peanuts on the corner than to be caught in a business that grieves the Holy Ghost, breaks the vase and shatters the mirror. Pleasures are for a pleasure mad people. Rome perished from bread and circuses.

Rome, that has given us a language and laws and literature and standards, believed it would never die, yet went down like a great rotten tree. Before whom did Rome go down? Rome went down by the pagan hordes from the North, the Huns, the Longbards and the rest of the vandals. People unworthy to carry their shoes, or black them. Rome did not die by military conquest from without; Rome died from bread and circuses and pleasure and divorce and fun and too much of everything. She got fat and weak; and when she was fat and weak, she died.

It is the way with churches and the way with you if you do not look out. It is also the way with countries. I say that nothing should permit us or hinder us, not fear itself, because is there anything more fearful than failure before God?

What shall we do then? We ought to amend our ways. "Thus saith the Lord of hosts, the God of Israel, amend your ways and your doings, and I will cause you to dwell in this place. But if ye trust not in lying words, saying The temple of the Lord, The temple of the Lord, The temple of the Lord, are these." This is our Christian religion. If you thoroughly amend your ways and your doings, then God will cause you to dwell in this place in the land that He gave your fathers forever and ever. So let us amend our giving and our praying, our relationships to others, our personal discipline, our prayer lives. Let us amend our ways before God that we might be a pure people completely acceptable to God; for no pure man can ever be defeated. No pure church can ever perish.

Prayer

O Lord Jesus, we remember Thy words back there where one of Thy churches allowed her love to cool off, Thou didst reach down and remove her candlestick, and not a trace was left of that church in that city. O Christ, we would seek before Thee tonight a perpetual witness. We seek that we should so amend our ways that Thou canst give us a second year, a second decade, a second scroll of years. But until Thy holy Son comes from heaven, the light will shine from this place. Not only around the neighborhood but also to New Guinea and Peru and Brazil and Japan and to all, wherever men need to hear the gospel. O God, we pray Thee, help us that we may amend our ways and begin to be and do that for which we were created. Now we are looking to Thee for help, Lord; we expect Thee to bless us; we want Thee to do it. Amen.

Maintaining a Vibrant Worship Lifestyle

And I John saw these things, and heard them. And when I had heard and seen, I fell down to worship before the feet of the angel which showed me these things. Then saith he unto me, See thou do it not: for I am thy fellowservant, and of thy brethren the prophets, and of them which keep the sayings of this book: worship God.

Revelation 22:8-9

Throughout this series, I have maintained that worship is not an event but a lifestyle. The more we treat worship as an event, the more it becomes a caricature of God's intention, and is unacceptable to Him. To maintain a lifestyle of worship, we must attend to it on a daily basis. If you regulate worship to a once-a-week event, you really do not understand it, and it will take a low priority in your life.

By nature, worship is not some performance we do, but a Presence we experience. Unless in our worship we have experienced the Presence of God, it cannot rightly be called Christian worship. I have pointed out that there can be worship apart from God, but such is not Christian worship. It is my contention that once we experience the actual Presence of God, we will lose all interest in cheap Christianity with all its bells and whistles vainly trying to compete with the world.

For worship to be a vital part of everyday life, it must be systematically and carefully nurtured.

Let me offer a few suggestions to help along the way. At this point, it is important to stay clear of all those sterile, mechanical regimens that think one size fits all. All of us are different, and although we are walking along the same path, we have different personalities. A few essentials need to be a part of our daily walk to maintain a vibrant life of worship. These are a few things that have helped me in my journey along the way with God.

Quiet

I put quietness first because unless we can find a place without distraction, the rest is undermined. We must withdraw from the world and find our repose in God. In such a frantic world as ours, it is almost impossible to find any quietness. Our world is riddled with noise of all kinds and intensity. Not only in the world, but increasingly the church itself echoes with noise and commotion. Finding a quiet corner to get away is a great challenge but well worth it.

When I first became a Christian, it was difficult to find a quiet place. Eventually I found refuge in a corner of our basement where I could focus on worship without interruption. Those were delightful times of fellowship with God and laid the foundation for not only my walk with God but also my ministry in the days to come.

I firmly believe it is important that we get still and wait on God. And it is best that we get alone, preferably with our Bible outspread before us. I usually have my *King James Bible*, but I do not think the version is that important. The important thing is to get alone with the Word of God. Then in the quietness of the moment, and as we draw near to God, we will begin to hear Him speak in our hearts. This is the most important part of our initial walk with God. To follow God arbitrarily is one thing, but I take great pleasure in the Scripture that says, "He that hath ears to hear, let him hear" what the Spirit sayeth (Luke 8:8). The saints of old always followed that voice. They got quiet enough to hear that "still, small voice of God" speaking to them.

For the average believer, the progression will be something like this: first, a sound as of a Presence walking in the garden; then a voice, more intelligible, but still far from clear. Then the happy moment when the Spirit begins to illuminate the Scriptures, and that which had been only a sound, or at best a voice, now becomes an intelligible word—as warm, intimate and clear as the word of a dear friend. Then will come life and light, and best of all, ability to see and rest in and embrace Jesus Christ as Savior and Lord and All.

The key here is to wait patiently and quietly on God. There is no need to rush. Noise is the enemy of the soul; and in our noise-enriched culture, it may take some doing, but the result is well worth the effort. Wait until He breaks through the tough exterior of your consciousness.

Cultivating quietness is a missing discipline in today's Christian church. There seems to be a wretched conspiracy in many churches to rob the saints of the quietness necessary to nurture their inner life, which is hid in Christ in God. The old saints would practice what they called "tarrying." They would get on their knees and tarry in God's presence until the light broke in their heart. Sometimes it took all night, but the wait was well worth it.

Scripture

All worship should begin with the Bible. This divine roadmap will lead us to God. It has been a neat trick of the devil to confuse us with a variety of translations. The Christian community is divided by which translation is the right one. I suggest that you settle this matter once for all in your own mind, no matter what it takes, and press on in spiritual growth and maturity. Then put the Bible in a prominent place in your daily life and allow nothing to interfere with reading it and meditating on it.

Our reading here should not be a marathon, but a slow, deliberate soaking in of its message. Bible reading calendars are no help here. There are times when one verse or even a phrase will strangely draw us. It would be impossible to go on until that Scripture has done its work in our heart. Do not faint here. Allow that Scripture to marinate in your mind and heart as long as it feeds your soul. God is speaking, and He deserves our utmost respect and attention. Often we regiment ourselves to a daily Bible reading schedule and hurry on in our reading to keep up. The importance of reading the Bible is not reading but fellowship with the Author. The proper reading of the Bible must be in the same Spirit that authored it.

I like to memorize portions of Scripture, especially the psalms of David. Charles Spurgeon used to say that we should read our Bibles until our blood became bibline. I like that. Memorizing the great passages of Scripture will go a long way in meditating on God, especially in the nighttime. "Thy Word have I hid in mine heart . . ." (Ps. 119:11) the psalmist said, and he knew something of delighting in the presence and fellowship of God.

Prayer

In your prayer life, quickly move beyond the idea of "getting things" from God. Prayer is not technical in the sense that if we go through the right motions, say the right words, automatically our prayer is answered. Our aim in prayer is not simply "getting our prayers answered." Here, we go beyond all that and luxuriate in the overwhelming presence of God. Prayer is not a monologue where we tell God what we think or want. Rather, it is a dialogue between two friends; an intimate fellowship that more often than not surpasses words. Words can be clumsy and grossly inadequate to express sufficiently how we feel. As the mystics and saints have encouraged, begin practicing the presence of God. This is not merely an exercise in imagination but the ecstatic joy of fellowship. Once you lose yourself in rapturous prayer, you will never go back to prayer by routine.

The key to prayer is simply praying. As we engage the God of the universe, our hearts are stretched upward in adoring wonder and admiration, resulting in spontaneous worship. Our heart always responds to that heavenly pull. This kind of praying is contagious and, thankfully, dangerous to spiritual status quo.

Hymns

I must confess that I am an ardent lover of hymns. In my library, I value a collection of old hymnals. Often, on the way to an appointment, I will grab one of these hymnals to read and meditate. After the Bible, the next most valuable book is a hymnal. But do not get one that is less than a hundred years old! Let any new Christian spend a year prayerfully meditating on the hymns of Watts and Wesley alone, and he will become a fine theologian. Then read a balanced diet of the Puritans and the Christian mystics, and the result will be more wonderful than you could dream.

The old hymnal is invaluable in my personal walk with God. This may be the most difficult. For a variety of reasons, many have tossed the hymnbook aside or at least have ignored it. It has been a successful ploy of the enemy to separate us from those lofty souls who reveled in the rarified atmosphere of God's presence. I suggest you find a hymnbook and learn how to use it. Perhaps one reason the hymnal has fallen out of favor with many is that we do not know how to read or sing a hymn. We are not taught in our churches the great hymns of the church; consequently, many Christians are the poorer, spiritually speaking.

Devotional Reading:
The Mystics and Saints

Apart from the Scriptures, which should be paramount in our daily walk with God, some devotional works of bygone saints can help us on our way. I am not thinking of those one-page daily devotionals popular with many people today. They may have some value for those just beginning their spiritual pilgrimage, but the growing Christian needs strong meat. If we are to mature in our Christian experience, we must have food to strengthen us for the journey.

In my search for God, I quite naturally was led to the Christian mystics. As a young Christian, I had never heard of them nor saw any of their books in the bookstore. A retired missionary thoughtfully placed into my hands one of these old Christian books and I was immediately in love. I discovered that these great saints were uncontrollably in love with God. My love and appreciation for these writers sprang out of my own heart's deep longing after and thirsting for God. These people knew God in a way that I did not, and I wanted to know what they knew about God and how they came to know it.

Certainly, in my admiration for these writers, I by no means endorsed everything they did or taught. I early learned that a hungry bee could get nectar out of any old flower and turn it into honey. For me, it was their utter devotion to God along with the ability to share their spiritual insights and observations that I valued. They assisted me in my walk with God as no other writers even of my day have. And, after all, that is all that really matters. I cannot place too much emphasis on the contemplation of divine things, which will result in the God-conscious life. These old mystics did just that for me.

Some have chided me about my affection for some of these old mystic friends of mine. I have learned to live above that. For me, I only require that a person must know God other than by hearsay. The intimacy of their relationship with God is all that truly matters. If a writer only has information to offer that he has obtained by research, I will pass on him. Give me the writer who has the passion and fire of God in his soul, which flows onto the page.

By "mystic," I simply mean that personal spiritual experience common to the saints of Bible times and well known to multitudes of persons in the postbiblical era. I am referring to the evangelical mystic who has been taught in the Christian Scriptures. He walks the high road of truth where walked of old prophets and apostles, and where down the centuries walked martyrs, reformers, Puritans, evangelists and missionaries of the cross. He differs from the ordinary orthodox Christian only because he experiences his faith down in the depths of his sentient being, while the other does not. He exists in a world of spiritual reality. He is quietly, deeply and sometimes almost ecstatically aware of the presence of God in his own nature and in the world around him. His religious experience is something elemental, as old as time and acquaintance with God by union with the eternal Son. It is to know that which passes knowledge.

Simplify Your Life

The average Christian's life is cluttered with all sorts of activities. We have more going on than we can keep up and still maintain our inner life with God. Some things need to be rooted out of our daily schedule in order to make room for that one essential thing in our life, the worship of God. Too many things in our life just suck the life out of us and are not essential to wholesome living. We find ourselves rushing through the devotional aspects of our life to give predominance to mere activities. Work without worship is totally unacceptable to God. It would be a good practice to go through your schedule once a month and find one thing to eliminate. Put it on the altar and see how God will respond. It would not be long until the most important thing in your life will be your personal worship of God.

Friendships

This I leave for last because it has the most potential danger. Your friends will either make or break your deeper walk with Christ. We must carefully choose our friends in this regard. Although it is not necessary to be rude, some friends will need to be marginalized to lessen the damage to our inner life. At times, we are thrown in with friends who are carnal in nature and frivolous in life. It is easy for our friends to distract us from our walk with Christ and from maintaining a vibrant life of worship. Often we will have to leave our friends behind in order to concentrate on our Friend.

Cultivate friendships with those who have made He who is the Friend of sinners their constant Companion.

These simple things will go a long way in maintaining a vibrant life of worship and praise. If what we believe does not make God more real to us, if it does not make us more Christlike in every aspect of our life, of what value is it? The maintaining of our worship is a responsibility we cannot shirk. It must be paramount in our daily life. The effect of all this is seen in, "But we all, with open face beholding as in a glass the glory of the Lord, are changed into the same image from glory to glory, even as by the Spirit of the Lord" (2 Cor. 3:18).

May God grant us a desire for God that supersedes all other desires.

Prayer

Dear heavenly Father, the world is very evil, times are waxing late and we are running out of time. Oh, God, lay hold of us. We pray that we may have eyes to see and ears to hear and hearts to understand. We pray that we may be saved from the routine and rut. We pray that we may have eyes inside and outside, anointed understanding. Help us, Lord, for Christ's sake. Amen.

Follow Tozer's new writings on Twitter at
http://twitter.com/tozeraw

A.W. TOZER:
THE AUTHORIZED BIOGRAPHY

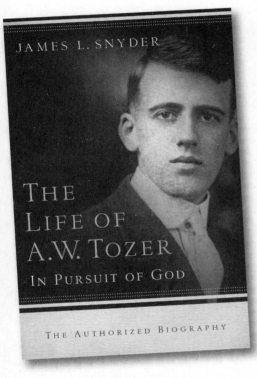

THE LIFE OF A.W. TOZER
James L. Snyder
ISBN 978.08307.46941
ISBN 08307.46943

To understand the ministry of A.W. Tozer, it is important to know who he was, including his relationship with God. In *The Life of A.W. Tozer,* James Snyder lets us in on the life and times of a deep thinker who was not afraid to "tell it like it is" and never compromised his beliefs. A.W. Tozer's spiritual legacy continues today as his writings challenge readers to a deeper relationship and worship of God in reverence and adoration. Here is Tozer's life story, from boyhood to his conversion at the age of 17, to his years of pastoring and writing more than 40 books (at least two of which are regarded as Christian classics and continue to appear on bestseller lists today). Examining Tozer's life will allow you to learn from a prophet who had much to say against the compromises he observed in contemporary Christian living and the hope he found in his incredible God.